THE AWAKENING OF FAITH

The Classic Exposition of
Mahayana Buddhism

ASVAGHOSA

Translated by Teitaro Suzuki

DOVER PUBLICATIONS, INC.
Mineola, New York

Bibliographical Note

This Dover edition, first published in 2003, is an unabridged republication of the work originally published in 1900 by The Open Court Publishing Company, Chicago, under the title *Açvaghosha's Discourse on the Awakening of Faith in the Mahâyâna.* The frontispiece of the original edition has been moved to the inside front cover of this book. The more common spelling of the author's name has been used on the covers, title page, and running heads, but the original form has been retained in the body of this book.

Library of Congress Cataloging-in-Publication Data

Asvaghosa.
[Mahayanasraddhotpadasastra. English]
The Awakening of faith : the classic exposition of Mahayana Buddhism / Asvaghosha ; translated by Teitaro Suzuki
p. cm.
Originally published: Açvaghosha's discourse on the awakening of faith in the Mahâyâna. Chicago : Open Court Publishing Co., 1900.
ISBN 0-486-43141-X (pbk.)
1. Mahayana Buddhism—Doctrines—Early works to 1800. I. Suzuki, Daisetz Teitaro, 1870-1966. II. Title.

BQ2992.E5S95 2003
294.3'42042—dc22

2003055479

Manufactured in the United States of America
Dover Publications, Inc., 31 East 2nd Street, Mineola, N.Y. 11501

PUBLISHER'S PREFACE.

AÇVAGHOSHA is the philosopher of Buddhism. His treatise on *The Awakening of Faith* is recognised by all Northern
schools and sects as orthodox and used even
to-day in Chinese translations as a text-book
for the instruction of Buddhist priests.

The original Sanskrit text has not been
found as yet, and if it should not be discovered
somewhere in India or in one of the numerous
libraries of the Buddhist vihâras, it would be
a great loss; for then our knowledge of Açvaghosha's philosophy would remain limited to
its Chinese translation.

Açvaghosha's treatise on *The Awakening
of Faith* is a small booklet, a monograph of
the usual size of Chinese fascicles, comprising
in its Chinese dress no more than about
10,800 characters, and may be read through
in a few hours. But the importance of this
monograph stands in no relation to its brev-

ity, and it is very strange that no translation
of it has appeared as yet in any European language. I was therefore exceedingly glad that
Mr. Teitaro Suzuki, a Japanese Buddhist and
a disciple of the Rev. Shaku Soyen, the distinguished Abbot of Kamakura, who was one
of the delegates of the Parliament of Religions at Chicago in 1893, undertook the work
of rendering Açvaghosha's monograph into
English form. I watched the progress of his
translation and my interest in the work increased the more I became familiar with the
thoughts of the great philosopher of Buddhism. Not only is my own interpretation
of Buddhism, as stated in the *Gospel of Buddha* and elsewhere, here fully justified, but
there are striking similarities between the
very terms of Açvaghosha's system and expressions which I have used in my own philosophical writings. The main coincidence
is the idea of Suchness, which is pure form,
or the purely formal aspect of things, deter-
mining their nature according to mathematical and mechanical laws.[1]

[1] This coincidence of some salient points need of course not
exclude disagreements in other important matters.

Suchness, according to Açvaghosha, is the cosmic order or *Gesetzmässigkeit* of the world; it is the sum total of all those factors which shape the universe and determine the destinies of its creatures. It is the norm of existence and is compared to a womb in which all things take shape and from which they are born. It is Plato's realm of ideas and Goethe's "Mothers" of the second part of *Faust*.

Suchness which in its absolute sense means the total system of the abstractly formal laws, including the moral order of the universe, is contrasted with the realm of Birth and Death. This realm of Birth and Death, is the material world of concrete objects. While Suchness is the domain of the universal, the realm of Birth and Death is the domain of the particular; and it is characteristic of the Mahayana school that the bodily, the particular, the concrete is not rejected as a state of sin, but only characterised as impure or defiled, imperfect, and implicated with sorrow and pain, on account of its limitedness and the illusions which naturally attach to it.

Suchness and the realm of Birth and Death

are not two hostile empires but two names of
the same thing. There is but one world with
two aspects describing two opposed phases of
one and the same existence. These two aspects form a contrast, not a contradiction.
Suchness (or the good law, the normative fac-
tor) dominates the realm of Birth and Death,
which latter therefore, in a certain sense, belongs to Suchness throughout in its entirety
as well as in its details.

But sentient beings are apt to overlook the
significance of the universal, for the senses
depict only the particular. Thus to a superficial consideration of sensual beings, the world
presents itself as a conglomeration of isolated
objects and beings, and the unity that consists
in the oneness of law which dominates all, is
lost sight of. It is the mind (or spiritual insight into the nature of things) which traces
the unity of being and learns to appreciate
the significance of the universal.

Universals, i. e., those factors which constitute the suchness of things are not sub-
stances, not entities, but relations, pure forms,
or determinants, i. e., general laws. Thus

they are not things, but ideas; and the most important one among them, the suchness of man or his soul, is not a concrete self, an ât-man, but "name and form."

It is well known what an important rôle the denial of the existence of the âtman plays in the Abhidharma, and we need not repeat here that it is the least understood and most misrepresented doctrine of Buddhism.

Thus the essential feature of existence, of that which presents itself to the senses, is not the material, but the formal; not that which makes it concrete and particular, but that which constitutes its nature and applies generally; not that which happens to be here, so that it is this, but that which makes it to be thus; not its Thisness, but its Suchness.

Particularity is not denounced as evil, but it is set forth as limited; and we might add (an idea which is not expressed in the Mahâ-yâna, but implied) that the universal would be unmeaning if it were not realised in the particular. Absolute Suchness without reference to the world of concrete Particularity is like a Pratyekabuddha, and the Pratyeka-

buddha, a sage whose wisdom does not go out
into the world to seek and to save, is regarded
as inferior to the Bodhisattvas, who with inferior knowledge combine a greater love and
do practical work that is of help to their
fellow beings.

How highly Particularity is considered appears from the Mahayana picture in which it
stands contrasted to Universality on perfectly
equal terms.[1]

The world-process starts in ignorance,
perhaps through ignorance or at least through
some commotion void of enlightenment, but
from the start it is enveloped by the good law
of cosmic order. Suchness, the norm of being,
guides its steps. It is shaped in the womb of
the Tathâgata and is in the progress of evolution more and more tinged, or, as Açvaghosha
says, perfumed, with the cognition of Suchness. Thus life will necessarily march onward
to Buddhahood, actualising in the course of
its development the eternal in the transient,
the omnipresent in the special, the universal
in the concrete and particular, and unchange-

[1] See the inside front cover.

able perfection in the imperfect haphazards of
the kaleidoscopic world of changes, in which
things originate by being compounded, and
perish according to the law that all compounds
are doomed to dissolution. Hence it becomes
apparent that the realm of Birth and Death is
the realisation only of that which in itself is
immortal; it is the appearance in time and
space, the actualisation, the materialisation,
the incarnation, of that which is everlasting
and permanent in the absolute sense. Says
Goethe:

> "Alles Vergängliche
> Ist nur ein Gleichniss,
> Das Unzulängliche
> Hier wird's Ereigniss."

The reading of Açvaghosha's treatise may
in some of its parts present difficulties, and
Western thinkers would undoubtedly express
themselves in other terms than this thinker of
India who lived almost two thousand years
ago; but the underlying ideas of his philosophy will be found simple enough, if the
reader will take the trouble patiently to consider the significance of every sentence in its
relation to the whole system.

PAUL CARUS.

TRANSLATOR'S PREFACE.

THE study of Buddhism has recently made gigantic strides, on this side of the Atlantic as well as on the other. Not only is the importance of the science of comparative religion making itself felt, but the advance of our Pali and Sanskrit knowledge has greatly contributed to a better understanding of things Oriental. Even Christians who were without sympathy for "heathen" religions have now taken up the study of Buddhism in earnest. Nevertheless, it appears to me that the teachings of Sakyamuni are not yet known in their full significance and that they do not yet command just appreciation. Though intolerant critics lose no chance of vigorously and often wrongly attacking the weak points of Buddhism, which are naturally seen at the surface, clear-sighted people have been very slow to perceive its innermost truth. This is especially the case with the Mahayana school.

The main reasons for this are, in my opinion, evident. While the canonical books of the Hinayana Buddhism have been systematically preserved in the Pali language, those of the Mahayana Buddhism are scattered promiscuously all over the fields and valleys of Asia and in half a dozen different languages. Further, while most of the Sanskrit originals have been destroyed, their translations in Tibetan, Mongolian, and Chinese have never been thoroughly studied. And, lastly, the Mahayana system is so intricate, so perplexingly abstruse, that scholars not accustomed to this form of thought and expression are entirely at a loss to find their way through it.

Among the false charges which have been constantly poured upon the Mahayana Buddhism, we find the following: Some say, "It is a nihilism, denying God, the soul, the world and all"; some say, "It is a polytheism: Avalokiteçvâra, Târa, Vajrapâni, Mañjuçrî, Amitâbha, and what not, are all worshipped by its followers"; still others declare, "It is nothing but sophistry, quibbling, hair-splitting subtlety, and a mocking of the innermost yearnings of humanity "; while those who attack it from the historical side proclaim, "It is not the genuine teaching of Buddha; it is on the contrary the pure invention of Nâgârjuna, who devised the system by ingeniously mixing up his negative philosophy with the non-âtman theory of his predecessor "; or, "The Mahayana is a queer mixture of the Indian mythology that grew most freely in the Tantric period, with a degenerated form of the noble ethical teachings of primitive Buddhism." Though no one who is familiar with Mahayanistic ideas will admit these one-sided and superficial judgments, the majority of people are so credulous as to lend their ear to these falsified reports and to believe them.

The present English translation of Açvaghosha's principal work is therefore dedicated to the Western public by a Buddhist from Japan, with a view to dispelling the denunciations so ungraciously heaped upon the Mahayana Buddhism. The name of Açvaghosha is not very well known to the readers of this country, but there is no doubt that he was the first champion, promulgator, and expounder of this doctrine, so far as we can judge from all our available historical records. Besides, in this book almost all the Mahayanistic thoughts, as distinguished from the other religious systems in India, are traceable, so that we can take it as the representative text of this school. If the reader will carefully and patiently go through the entire book, unmindful of its peculiar terminology and occasional obscureness, I believe he will be amply and satisfactorily repaid for his labor, and will find that the underlying ideas are quite simple, showing occasionally a strong resemblance to the Upanishad philosophy as well as to the Samkhya system, though of course retaining its own independent thought throughout.

In conclusion let me say a word about the difficulty of translating such an abstruse religio-philosophic discourse as the present text. It is comparatively easy to translate works of travels or of historical events or to make abstracts from philosophical works. But a translator of the Mahayanistic writings, which are full of specific phraseology and highly abstruse speculations, will find himself like a

wanderer in some unknown region, not knowing how to obtain any communicable means
to express what he perceives and feels. To
reproduce the original as faithfully as possible
and at the same time to make it intelligible
enough to the outside reader, who has perhaps
never come in contact with this form of
thought, the translator must be perfectly acquainted with the Mahayanistic doctrine as it
is understood in the East, while he must not
be lacking in adequate knowledge of Western
philosophy and mode of thinking. The present translator has done his best to make the
Mahayanistic thoughts of Açvaghosha as clear
and intelligible as his limited knowledge and
lack of philosophic training allow him. He is
confident, however, that he has interpreted the
Chinese text correctly. In spite of this, some
errors may have crept into the present translation, and the translator will gladly avail
himself of the criticisms of the Mahayana
scholars to make corrections in case a second
edition of the work is needed.

TEITARO SUZUKI.

LA SALLE, ILL., May, 1900.

TABLE OF CONTENTS:

NOTE.

The method of transliteration for Sanskrit words adopted in the present book is one used in Whitney's *Sanskrit Grammar*, but from lack of type *sh* has been substituted for *s̩*, *r* for the vowel *r̩*, *n* for all the different kinds of nasal *n*'s, and *m* for *ṁ*. Further, no distinction has been made in the footnotes between the dentals and the cerebrals; *c* and *ç* are also often used indiscriminately there.

As to the method of transliteration for Chinese words, almost every Sinologue has his own; but the one used in this book is that of Sir T. Wade, which I think has been adopted more generally than others.

INTRODUCTION.

AÇVAGHOSHA, the first expounder of the Mahâyânistic doctrine and one of the deepest thinkers among the Buddhist patriarchs, is known to most
Western Buddhist scholars simply as the author of
the *Buddha-caritakâvya*,[1] the famous poem on the life
of Buddha. The accounts of his life and of the significance of his philosophy are so few that the important influence exercised by him upon the development
of the Mahâyâna Buddhism has been left almost entirely unnoticed. That he was one of the most eminent leaders among earlier Buddhists; that he was in
some way or other connected with the third convocation in Kashmir, probably presided over by the Bhikshu Parçva; that he had a wonderful poetical genius
which rendered great service in the propagation of
Buddhism,—these facts sum up almost all the knowledge possessed by scholars about Açvaghosha. The
reason why he is not known as he ought to be, is principally that the Sanskrit sources are extremely mea-

[1] *The Sacred Books of the East*, Vol. XLIX. Beal's English
translation of the Chinese translation *The Fo sho hing tsan king*,
S. B. E., Vol. XIX.

gre, while the accounts obtainable from Chinese and Tibetan traditions are confusing and full of legends.

This fact has led Professor Kern to say that Açvaghosha was not an historical man, but a personification of Kâla, a form of Çiva.[1] But the sources from which the Professor draws his conclusion are rather too meagre and I fear are not worth serious consideration. In the following pages we shall see by what traditions Açvaghosha's life is known to the Buddhists of the East.

DATE.

Let us first decide the date, which varies according to different authorities from three hundred to six hundred years after the Parinirvâna of Buddha.

1. The *Li tai san pao chi* (*fas..* 1),[2] quoting the Record of the Sarvâstivâdin school, says: "Açvaghosha Bodhisattva was born a Brahman in Eastern India some three hundred years after the Nirvâna. After he abandoned his worldly life, he refuted all the doctrines held by the tîrthakas (heathen),[3] and writing

---

[1] *Der Buddhismus und seine Geschichte in Indien*, authorised German translation, Leipsic, 1884, Vol. II., p. 464.

[2] 歷代三寶記 *Records of the Triratna Under Successive Dynasties*, compiled by 費長房 Fe Chang-fang, A. D. 597; 15 *fasciculi*.

[3] Tîrthaka, which literally means "ascetics," was first applied to a definite sect, viz., the naked ascetics of the Jains, but was later on extended to all dissenters and has therefore been translated "heretics or heathen." The Chinese translation of the term literally means "[followers of] a doctrine other than Buddhism."

the *Mahâ-alamkâra-çâstra*[1] in several hundred verses (*ghâtâs*) greatly propagated the teachings of Buddha."

2. Hui-yuen[2] states in his commentary (*fas.* 1) on the *Mahâ-prajñâ-pâramitâ-çâstra*,[3] on the authority of Kumârajîva 鳩摩羅什 (A. D. 339–413), that Açvaghosha flourished about three hundred and seventy years after the Nirvâna.

3. In the *Life of Vasubandhu*,[4] Açvaghosha is mentioned as a contemporary of Kâtyâyana who is said in the same book to have been living in the fifth century after the Nirvâna.

4. The writer[5] of the preface to the second Chinese translation of the *Mahâyâna-çraddhotpâda-çâstra*[6] says that this Çâstra "is the deepest of the Mahâyâna texts. Five hundred years after the Nirvâna, Açvaghosha appeared in the world. He was numbered.

---

[1] Translated into Chinese by Kumârajîva, circa A. D. 405. 15 *fas.*

[2] 慧遠 A. D. 333–416. The leader of the Pai lien she (White Lotus Society), first Sukhâvatî sect movement in China.

[3] *Treatise on the Great Wisdom-Perfection*, by Nâgârjuna. A Chinese translation by Kumârajîva, A. D. 402–405. 100 *fas.*

[4] The original Sanskrit author is unknown. The present Chinese translation is by Paramârtha who came to China from Western India A. D. 546.

[5] The writer's name is not mentioned there, nor the date; but judging from the knowledge he shows in treating the subject, as we shall see later, he must have been living either at the time of this second translation or immediately after it.

[6] *Discourse on the Awakening of Faith in the Mahâyâna*, the principal work of Açvaghosha.

among the four suns [of Buddhists], and his teachings stood most prominently [among the doctrines prevailing] in the five countries of India."

5. Sang-ying[1] states in his preface to the Chinese translation of the *Mahá-prajñá-páramitá-çástra* that Açvaghosha appeared towards the end of the period of Orthodoxy, i. e., five hundred years after the Nirvâna.

6. The *Fu tsou t'ung chi*[2] (Vol. V.) says that it was the fulfilment of the Tathâgata's prophecy that six hundred years after the Nirvâna the Dharma was transmitted to Açvaghosha.

7. This six hundred year prophecy is adopted as if it were an unquestionable fact, by Fa-tsang,[3] a learned commentator of the *Çraddhotpâdaçástra (Discourse on the Awakening of Faith)*.

8. Chih-k'ai 智愷, who was the copyist for Paramârtha when he translated the *Çraddhotpâdaçástra*, also adheres to the six hundred year tradition in his preface to the book just mentioned, saying that some six hundred years after the Nirvâna of the Tathâgata, many devilish heretical leaders clamorously protested their false doctrines against the good law of Buddha,

---

[1] 僧叡 A. D. 362–439. One of the four famous disciples of Kumârajîva.

[2] 佛祖統記 A history of Buddhism, compiled by Chih-p'an 志盤, a Chinese priest, during the latter half of the thirteenth century. 54 *fas.*

[3] 643–712. A most prominent leader of the Avatamsaka sect in China.

when a Çrâmana of very high virtue, called Açvagho-sha, thoroughly versed in the philosophy of the Mahâ-yâna Buddhism and highly compassionate for those ignorant people, wrote this Discourse (the *Çraddhot-pâdaçâstra*), in order that he might increase the brilliancy of the Triratna, etc., etc.

9. The six hundred year tradition is very popular among Chinese and Japanese Buddhists. The *Fa tsu li tai tung tsai*[1] (*fas.* 5) also follows it.

10. The prophecy above referred to (see No. 8), which is doubtless a later invention, appears in the *Mahâmâyâ sûtra*[2] (*fas.* 2) as follows:

"After the death of Buddha, Mahâmâyâ asked Ânanda if Buddha had ever told him in his life anything concerning the future of Buddhism. Responding to this, Ânanda said: 'I heard one time Buddha say this with regard to the future decline of Buddhism: "After the Nirvâna Mahâkâçyapa with Ânanda will compile the Dharma-piṭaka, and when it is settled Mahâkâçyapa will enter into a Nirodha-samâpatti in the Lang chi shan [i. e., Mount of Wolf's Track, Kukkurapadagiri], and Ânanda too obtaining the fruit

---

[1] 佛祖歷代通載 *A History of Buddha and the Patriarchs Through Successive Dynasties*, by Nien chang 念常, A. D. 1333. 36 *fas.*

[2] The Sûtra is also called the *Sûtra on Buddha's Ascent to the Trayastrimsa Heaven, to Teach the Dharma to His Mother* 2 *fas.* A second Chinese translation by Shih T'an-ching 釋曇景 of the Ch'i dynasty 齊 (A. D. 479–502). His nationality and life both are unknown.

of enlightenment will in turn enter into Parinirvâna, when the right doctrine will be transmitted to Upagupta who will in an excellent manner teach the essence of the Dharma. . . . When five hundred years are passed [after Buddha's death] a Bhikshu named Pao-tien [Ratnadeva?] will in an excellent manner teach the essence of the Dharma, converting twenty thousand people and causing all sentient beings in the eight creations to awaken the Anuttarasamyak-sambodhicitta [most-perfect-knowledge-mind]. The right doctrine will then go to decline. When six hundred years [after Buddha's death] are expired, ninety different schools of the tîrthakas will arise and proclaiming false doctrines, each will struggle against the other to destroy the law of Buddha. Then a Bhikshu, Açvaghosha by name, will in an excellent manner teach the essence of the Dharma and defeat all the followers of the tîrthakas. When seven hundred years [after Buddha's death] are expired, a Bhikshu, Nâgârjuna by name, will in an excellent manner teach the essence of the Dharma, destroying the banner of false philosophy and lighting the torch of the right doctrine." ' "

11. Referring to the statement of the above mentioned Sûtra, Nâgârjuna, a famous Buddhist philosopher who wrote a commentary on Açvaghosha's work, called *Çraddhotpâdaçâstra*, claims that there were six Açvaghoshas at different times, to fulfil the prophecy of Buddha and that the author of the book on which

he writes a commentary[1] was one who appeared on earth according to the prophecy in the *Mahâmâyâ sûtra*. Nâgârjuna even states that he was a disciple of Açvaghosha, but the work itself is regarded as spu-

[1] The Sanskritised title is the *Mahâyâna-çâstra-vyâkhyâ*, trans. into Chinese by Pa-ti-mo-to 筏 提 摩 多, an Indian priest, A. D. 401–402. 10 *fas*. The statements in full run as follows:

"In all there were six Açvaghoshas, owing to different predictions in the sûtras; each of them appeared to fulfil his mission according to the necessity of the time, and there is no contradiction in them."

The author then proceeds to make particular references to those sûtras:

"When we examine all different predictions in the sûtras taught by Buddha through his whole life, we find six different [personages all called Açvaghosha]. What are those six? (1) According to the 大 乘 本 法 契 經 *Tai ch'êng pên fa ch'i ching* (*Mahâyânapûrvadharmasûtra?*) we have the following: When the peerless, great, enlightened, honored one was speaking about his intention of entering into Nirvâna, Açvaghosha rising from the seat knelt down, saluted Buddha's feet, and respectively joining his hands together turned towards Buddha, the world-honored one, and said this in verse: 'The peerless one whose heart is filled with great love and whose immeasurable virtues have been accumulated through æons which are like a boundless ocean, the Buddha, only on account of love and compassion for all sentient beings, now speaks about his entering into Nirvâna, and I and all the other members of the Saṃgha feel an unspeakable despair, utterly confused in mind and spirit. If even the world-honored one, full of great love, is going to another world, leaving his own children behind him, why then could not I who am not yet full of love and compassion go to another world following Buddha's steps? Who can blame me?' When finished uttering these words, Açvaghosha gazed at the pupil of Buddha's eye and gradually passed out of life. (2) The 變 化 功 德 契 經 *Pien 'hua kung tê ch'i ching* (*Vikriyâpunyasûtra?*) says: Then the Bhagavat said to Açvaghosha: 'Three hundred years after my Nirvâna thou shalt obtain an inspiration from me and with various methods (*upâya*)

rious, on account of some obvious contradictions, though the followers of the Mantra sect (*Shingonshyu*) insist on its genuineness, because they are anxious to have an ancient authority for their own mystic doctrines, which are here supported.

benefit and make happy all beings in coming generations. When thou dost not have any inspiration from me, thou canst not do this by thyself.' (3) The 摩訶摩耶契經 *Mahâmâyâsûtra* says as follows: 'When six hundred years are passed after the disappearance of the Tathâgata, ninety-six different schools of the tîrthakas will arise, and professing false doctrines, each will struggle against the other to destroy the law of Buddha. A Bhikshu called Açvaghosha, however, will in an excellent manner proclaim the essence of the Dharma and defeat all followers of the tîrthakas. (4) In the 常德三昧契經 *Ch'ang tê san mei ch'i ching* (*Sûtra on the Samâdhi of Eternal Merit*) we read: In the eight hundredth year after the Nirvâna there will be a wise man, Açvaghosha by name. Among the followers of the tîrthakas as well as those of Buddhism, he will refute all those who cherish heretical views and will establish the Dharma taught by Buddha. (5) In the 摩尼清淨契經 *Mo ni ch'ing ching ch'i ching* (*Manivimâlasûtra?*) is said thus: About one hundred years after the Nirvâna of Buddha, Açvaghosha Mahâsattva will appear on earth protect the right doctrine and safely hoist the banner of Buddhism. (6) In the 勝頂王契經 *Shêng ting wang ch'i ching* (*Crimûrdharâjasûtra?*) is said thus: On the seventeenth day after the enlightenment of Buddha there was a tîrthaka called 迦羅諾鳩尸摩 Chia-lo-no-chiu-shih-to (Kâlanakshiṭa?), who transforming himself into the figure of a great nâgarâja (i. e., snake-king) with 86,000 heads and 86,000 tongues, simultaneously proposed 86,000 contradicting questions and asked the Tathâgata [for the solution]. He then gave him a triple answer explaining all those paradoxes. The nâgarâja then proposed tenfold questions, again asking the Tathâgata [for their solution], to which he gave a hundredfold answers and explained their paradoxes. When this dialogue came to an end, Buddha said to the nagarâja: 'Very good, very good, O Açvaghosha Çrâmana! in order to guard the castle of the Dharma, thou hast assumed this form of destruction, estab-

Deeply absorbed in metaphysical speculation, the inhabitants of India paid very little attention to history, and whenever we endeavor to ascertain the date of important historical figures we are sure to find our way to certainty barred. So we cannot decide which of the conflicting traditions above enumerated is to be considered as authentic. When taken independently of other historical events which are connected with them and whose dates have been already fixed, they have no value whatever. Besides it should be observed, the chronology of Buddha, to which every one of the traditions makes reference, is as yet unsettled and must have been still more so at the time when those traditions were current in India as well as in China. If they differed as to the date of Buddha, they might have maintained the same date for Açvaghosha; no one can tell. We have to seek a light from another source.

Another group of traditions centering around Açvaghosha is his connexion with a most powerful king of Yüeh chih 月氏國, who established his extensive kingdom in Northwestern India. Who was this king? In the 雜寶藏經 *Tsa pao tsang ching* (*Samyuktaratna-*

lishing the doctrine of Buddha. Be patient, be patient, always discipline thyself in this way, always behave thyself in this way, do not go round in a small circle, but make a universal tour.' The nagârâja then abandoning his assumed beast-form revealed his own real character and approaching the peerless, honored one and saluting him said rejoicingly in verse, etc., etc. This is the sixth Açvaghosha."

pitaka-sûtra?)[1], *fas.* 7, we read: "A king of Tukhâra, Candana Kanishṭha[2] (or Kanîta? Chinese 旃檀罽昵吒 *chan-tan-chi-ni-ch'a*) had a close friendship with three wise men: the first one was a Bodhisattva, called Açvaghosha; the second, a minister of state called Mo-cha-lo (Maṭhara or Madara?); the third, an experienced physician called Chê-lo-chia (Caraka). With these three the king was on most intimate terms and treated them with the utmost cordiality, permitting them to approach his person. Açvaghosha said [one day] to him that if he [the king] would follow his advice, he would obtain in his coming life everything that was good, eternally put an end to all his misfortunes and forever be free from evil." . . .[3]

[1] *Sutra on the Casket of Miscellaneous Jewels.* The original Sanskrit author is unknown. Translated into Chinese by Chi-chia-yeh (吉迦夜 Kimkara?) of the Western country and T'an-yao 曇曜, A. D. 472. 8 *fas.* The original text is said to have existed at the time when the *Chêng-yüan Catalogue* 貞元錄 was compiled (A. D. 785–804) by Yüan-chao 圓照, a Buddhist priest of the Tang 唐 dynasty (A. D. 618–907).

[2] Does Kanishṭha, which literally means "youngest," refer to the youngest of the three brothers who successively governed the Tukhâra district of India? If so, there is no question about the identity of him and King Kanishka.

[3] The *Fu fa tsang ch'uan* (*Transmission of the Dharma-pitaka*), *fas.* 5, also seems to refer to the same tradition, for it is stated that when a king of Tukhâra (probably Kanishka) was very much afflicted on account of his having committed many atrocious deeds in the war with Parthia (Eastern Persia), Açvaghosha told him that if he would follow the Dharma with a sincere heart, his sin would gradually be attenuated; and also that the same king had a physician called Caraka "who thoroughly understood phar-

Açvaghosha's relation with King Candana Kanishṭha (or Kanîta? Chinese Chi-ni-ch'a) is told also in
the *Fu fa tsang yin yüan ch'uan*,[1] *fas.* 5 :

"[At that time] the king of Tukhâra was very
powerful. He was called Candana Kanishṭha [or
Kanîta? Chinese Chi-ni-ch'a]. Being very ambitious
and bold, and far superior in courage to all his con-
temporaries, every country he invaded was sure to be
trampled down under his feet. So when he advanced
his four armies towards Pâṭaliputra [Hua shih ch'êng
in Chinese], the latter was doomed to defeat in spite
of some desperate engagements. The king demanded
an indemnity of 900,000,000 gold pieces, for which
the defeated king offered Açvaghosha, the Buddha-
bowl and a compassionate fowl, each being considered worth 300,000,000 gold pieces. The Bodhisattva
Açvaghosha had intellectual powers inferior to none;
the Buddha-bowl having been carried by the Tathâgata himself is full of merits; the fowl being of compassionate nature, would not drink any water with
worms in it,—thus all these having merits enough to
keep off all enemies, they are on that account worth

macy, and who was clever, learned, intelligent, elegant, meek, and
compassionate," etc.

[1] 付法藏因緣傳 *Accounts Relating to the Transmission of
the Dharmapitaka.* 6 *fas.* The original Sanskrit author is unknown. The third Chinese translation now existent is by Chi-
chia-yeh (Kimkara?) of the Western country, A. D. 472. The
original text is said to have been existing when the *Chêng yüan
Catalogue* (A. D. 785–804) was compiled.

900,000,000 gold pieces.[1] The king [of Tukhâra] was greatly pleased at receiving them, and immediately withdrawing his army from the land went back to his own kingdom."

We have the same legend stated in a brief biography[2] of Açvaghosha as follows:

"After that a king of the smaller Yüeh chih country [i. e., Tukhâra] in North India invaded the Middle country [i. e., Magadha]. When the besieging had continued for some time, the king of Central India sent a message [to the invader] saying: "If there be anything you want, I will supply it; do not disturb the peace of my people by thus long staying here,' to which this reply was given: 'If you really ask a surrender, send me 300,000,000 gold pieces; I will release you.' The [besieged] king said: 'Even this entire kingdom cannot produce 100,000,000 gold pieces, how can I supply you with 300,000,000?' The answer was: 'There are in your country two great treasures: (1) the Buddha-bowl,[3] (2) a Bhikshu of

[1] This is a comical feature of the legend, for if these treasures could ward off all enemies why did they not protect the unfortunate king of Pâtaliputra against Kanishtha?

[2] *Life of Açvaghosha* 馬鳴菩薩傳, translated into Chinese by Kumârajîva. Very short. The author is unknown. The original Sanskrit text is stated in the *Chêng yüan Catalogue* to have been existing at that time. Cf. Wassijew's *Buddhismus*, German edition, p. 231 et seq.

[3] Fa-hien 法顯 states that Kanishka (which is transliterated by him into Chinese Chi-ni-chia 罽貳迦, corresponding to Sanskrit Kanika) as if a different person from the king of Yüeh chih

wonderful talent (i. e., Açvaghosha). Give them to
me, they are worth 300,000,000 gold pieces.' The
[besieged] king said : 'Those two treasures are what
I most revere, I cannot give them up.' Thereupon
the Bhikshu said to the king in explanation of the
Dharma :

" 'All sentient beings are everywhere the same,
while Buddhism, deep and comprehensive, aims at
universal salvation, and the highest virtue of a great
man consists in delivering [all] beings. As our temporal administration is very liable to meet obstruc-
tions, even your rule does not extend itself outside of
this one kingdom. If you, on the other hand, propose
a wide propagation of Buddhism, you would naturally
be a Dharmarâja over the four oceans. The duty of
a Bhikshu is to save [all] the people and not to give
preference to one or the other. Merits lie in our
heart; truth makes no distinction. Pray, be far-
sighted, and do not think only of the present.'

"The king who was from the first a great admirer
of him, respectfully followed his advice and delivered
him to the king of Yüeh chih who returned with him
to his own kingdom."

Comparing all these traditions, we are naturally
led to the conclusion that Açvaghosha, who was numbered as one of the four suns [1] of Buddhism, must have

who invaded Gandhâra to get the Buddha-bowl. *Vide* Legge's
translation of Fa-hien, pp. 33 and 34.

[1] Hsüen-tsang's 玄 弉 , *Records of Western Countries*, Beal's
English translation, Vol. II., p. 302.

had a very powerful influence over the spiritual India
of the time, that the king who wished to have him as
a spiritual adviser must have been a very devoted Buddhist so as to accept a Bhikshu instead of an enor-
mous sum of money, and that such a devoted Buddhist
king, ruling over the vast domain which extended
from the bank of the Indus towards the lower Ganges,
must have been living sometime between the third
and sixth century after the Nirvâna, whatever the
authentic date of Buddha might be.   The next conclusion we can advance therefore will be the identification of this king who is called Candana Kanishṭha
or Kanîta in the above stories, with Kanishka,[1] the
originator of the third Buddhist convocation in Kashmir.

As to the difference of the name, we have to say
this.   While Hsüen-tsang's transliteration for Kanishka
is Chia-ni-shê-chia 迦膩色迦 which is quite an approximate reproduction of the original sounds, the Chinese
method of transliteration before his time by the so-
called "old translators" was rather irregular, loose
and therefore often misleading.   Add to this the liabil-
ity to error on the part of local dialects, and we do not
improperly identify Chi-ni-ch'a, with Kanishka, while
the former may be Sanskritised Kanishṭa or Kanîta.[2]

---

[1] A. D. 85–106, according to M. Müller.

[2] One objection to identifying Chi-ni-ch'a 罽呢吒 (Kanishṭha
or Kanîta) with Kanishka 迦膩色迦 is a single Chinese character
appearing in the *Mahâlamkâraçâstra* (*Book of Great Glory*), the
work ascribed to Açvaghosha.   In *fas.* 3 as well as *fas.* 6 of the

In further support of this view, we quote from the *Journal of the Buddhist Text Society*, Vol. I., Part 3, an article on King Kanishka, taken from a Tibetan source, which bears a more historical appearance than the legends above referred to. The abstract is:

"Kanishka, king of Palhâva and Delhi,[1] was born four hundred years after the Nirvâna. When he learned that Simha, king of Kashmir, abandoned the worldly life to become a Buddhist priest under the name of Sudarçana and obtained Arhatship, he went to Kashmir and heard a sermon delivered by Sudarçana.[2] At that time a Mahâyâna priest who held a most prom-

same book referring to Candana Kanishtha or Kanîta, the writer says: " 我昔甞聞旃檀罽昵吒 *Wo hsi ch'ang wên, chan-t'an chi-ni-châ wang*," i. e., "I heard of old that King Candana Kanishtha," etc. (in *fas.* 6., chia-ni-ch'a), etc., etc. The Chinese character *hsi* usually means "of yore" or "in olden times," but it also signifies the past indefinitely, near as well as distant. If we thus understand the term in the sense of "some time ago," or simply "once," there will be no difficulty in demonstrating that Açvaghosha was an elder contemporary of Kanishka, though we cannot apparently accept the Chinese tradition which says they were intimately known to each other. Because in that case Açvaghosha would not refer to the king in such a hearsay manner as stated in the book above mentioned. Taking all in all, this does not prevent us asserting that they were contemporaneous.

[1] Cf. A. Schiefner's German translation of Târanâtha's *History of Buddhism*, p. 89: "Nachdem König Çrîtschandra die Herrschaft ausgeübt hatte, waren viele Jahre vergangen, als im Westen im Lande Tili und Mälava ein an Jahren junger König Kanika in die Herrschaft gewählt wurde."

[2] Târanâtha's statement differs from this. According to him Kanika and Kanishka are not the same king, the former being that of Tili and Mâlava, while the latter that of Jâlamdhara. *Vide* pp. 58 and 90. Târanâtha might have confused them.

inent position in northern countries was called Açvaghosha. His influence in the spiritual world was as
incomparable as the temporal power of Kanishka who
conquered Kashmir and Jâlamdhara. The king sent
a message to Açvaghosha to come to his kingdom,
who, however, owing to his old age, could not accept
the invitation, but sent him a leading disciple of his
called Jñânayaça, accompanied with a letter treating
the essential points of Buddhism."[1]

Though the Tibetan tradition considerably differs
in many respects from the Chinese accounts above
mentioned, they both agree in this point that Açvaghosha and Kanishka had some intercourse, or that at
least they were contemporaneous and known to each
other. So we may take it as an established fact that
Açvaghosha, the author of the 大乘起信論 *Mahâyâna-
çraddhotpâda-çâstra* (*Discourse on the Awakening of
Faith in the Mahâyâna*), was living at the time of Kanishka.[2]

I do not think there is any need here to enumerate
all different opinions about the time of Kanishka,
which has been already approximately fixed by the
untiring investigation of European scholars, such as
Princep, Lassen, Cunningham, Wilson, Fergusson,

---

[1] Târanâtha also states this event (*Geschichte des Buddhismus*, p. 92). But the king is not Kanishka, but Kanika ; and the
name of the disciple is not Jñânayaça, but Dschnânakriya.

[2] A further corroboration of this view will be met with when
we treat later on of the conversion of Açvaghosha by Parçva or his
disciple Puṇyayaças.

Max Müller, and others.[1] So long as our present aim is to assign the time of Açvaghosha more definitely than stating vaguely some three or five hundred years after the Nirvâna of Buddha, suffice it to say that he lived at the time extending from the latter half of the first century before Christ to about 50 or 80 A. D. If we fix the date of Buddha's death in the fifth century before Christ, Açvaghosha must be said to have lived during the six hundredth year after the Nirvâna. At the very most his time cannot be placed later than the first century of the Christian era.

I have spared no pains, even at the risk of tediousness, in gathering all the information obtainable from Chinese sources relative to the date of Açvaghosha, because this date is of paramount importance when we enter into the discussion of the development of the Mahâyâna Buddhism, which is commonly and erroneously considered to be the sole work of Nâgârjuna.

NATIVITY AND PEREGRINATIONS.

There is not so much discordance in the traditions about the wanderings of Açvaghosha as about his date, though indeed we do not have as yet any means of ascertaining his birth-place, other than the statements

---

[1] Max Müller's opinion, as stated before, is that Kanishka lived A. D. 85–106; Lassen thinks the Gondopharean dynasty was succeeded by Kanishka, king of the Yüeh chih, about one hundred years before Christ; Princep places his reign during the first century A. D.; Cunningham thinks his consecration was 58 A. D.; Fergusson, 79 A. D.; Rhys Davids, about 10 A. D., etc.

of discordant authorities. According to Târanâtha,[1] he was a son of a rich Brahman called Samghaguhya who married the tenth and youngest daughter of a merchant in Khorta. As a youth, when thoroughly familiar with every department of knowledge, he went to Odiviça, Gaura, Tîrahuti, Kâmarûpa, and some other places, defeating everywhere his Buddhist opponents by his ingenious logic.

All these places are situated in Eastern India, and among the Chinese traditions the *Record of the Triratna* (*Li tai san pao chi*) as well as the *Accounts of Buddha and the Patriarchs* (*Fo tsu tung chi*) agree with Târanâtha in placing Açvaghosha's native land in the East; but the *Life of Vasubandhu* makes Açvaghosha a native of Bhâshita in Çrâvastî, while in Nâgârjuna's work, *the Mahdyânaçâstravydkhyâ* 釋摩訶衍論 (*Shih mo ho yen lun*), he is mentioned as having been born in Western India, Loka being the father and Ghonâ the mother. The *Record of Buddha and the Patriarchs Under Successive Dynasties* (*Fo tsu li tai t'ung tsai*) agrees with neither of the above statements, for it says (*fasciculi* 5): "The twelfth patriarch, Açvaghosha Mahâsattva was a native of Vârânasî." A further contradicting tradition is pointed out by Prof. S. Murakami in one of his articles on the history of Buddhism,[2] quoting the *Shittanzô* 悉曇藏 (*fas.* 1), which makes Açvaghosha a man of South India.

---

[1] *Geschichte des Buddhismus*, p. 90.

[2] The *Bukkyô Shirin*, Vol. I., No. 6.   1894.   Tokyo, Japan.

A majority of the traditions place his native country in East India; but there is no means of confirm-
ing these.   One thing, however, seems to be certain,
namely, that Açvaghosha was not born in the northern
part of India, which place is supposed by most Western Buddhist scholars to be the cradle of the Mahâyâna school.

Wherever the native country of Açvaghosha may
have been, both the Chinese and Tibetan records agree
that he made a journey to Central India, or Magadha.
It seems that every intellectual man in India, the people of which, living in affluence, were not occupied
with the cares of making a living, sought to gain
renown by dialectics and subtle reasonings, and Açvaghosha, as a Brahman whose "intellectual acquire-
ments were wonderfully deep," and whose "penetrating insight was matchless,"[1] could not resist the
temptation.   Not satisfied with his intellectual cam-
paign against commonplace Buddhists in his neighbor-
hood, who were crushed down as "rotten wood before
a raging hurricane,"[2] he went, according to a Chinese
tradition, to Pâṭaliputra, and according to the Tibetan,
to Nâlanda.   The *Life of Açvaghosha* evidently refers
to this fact when it states that Pârçva, the eleventh
patriarch and eventual teacher of Açvaghosha, on being informed of the paramount influence of the Brah-

[1] The *Transmission of the Dharmapitaka* (*Fu fa tsang
ch'uan, fas.* 5).

[2] The same as above.

man tîrthaka (i. e., Açvaghosha) in Central India and of the fact that his conquest over Buddhists had silenced the bell (*ghanta*) in some monastery (*vihâra*), journeyed from Northern India to convert the bitterest opponent into a faithful follower of Buddha. He adds that Açvaghosha left his home and lived henceforth in Central India. But according to the *Transmission of the Dharmapitaka* (*Fu fa tsang ch'uan, fas.* 5) we find Açvaghosha even after his conversion still in Pâtaliputra, from which he was taken by King Kanishka to the latter's own capital, Gandhâra, in the Northwest of India.

Thus all that we can say about the birth-place and wanderings of Açvaghosha is: (1) he was a Brahman by birth either of South, or of West, or of East, but not of North India ; (2) he acquired in Central India his highest reputation as a Brahman disputant, and, after his conversion, as the greatest Buddha follower of the time, intellectually as well as morally; (3) his later life was spent according to the Chinese authority in the North where he wrote probably the *Mahâlamkâra-sûtraçâstra* (*Book of Great Glory*) which describes matters mostly relating to Western India.

APPELLATIONS.

The author of the *Mahâyânaçraddhotpâdaçâstra* (*Discourse on the Awakening of Faith in the Mahâyâna*) is most commonly known in the Chinese Buddhist literature by the name of Açvaghosha. But according to his *Life* he was also called Kung-tê-jih 功德日 (i. e., merit-sun; in Sanskrit, Puṇyaditya?). For he was not only a philosopher, but a preacher and an organiser, for "while in North India he widely propagated the doctrine of Buddha, led and benefited the masses, and through good and excellent [missionary] methods perfected the merits of the people." The *Record of Buddha and the Patriarchs* (*Fo tsou t'ung tsai*), where it is stated that his other name was Kung-chang 功勝 (Puṇyaçrîka?), can be said almost to agree with the above. While thus no other name or appellation of his is known in China, Târanâtha mentions nine more names: Kâla (Time), Durdarsha (Hard-to-be-seen), Durdarshakâla (Hard-to-be-seen-time), Mâtṛceta (Mother-child), Pitṛceta (Father-child), Çûra (Hero), Dharmika-Subhûti (Virtuous-mighty), and Maticitra (Intelligence-bright).[1]

In I-tsing's *Correspondence from the South Sea* (*Nan hai chi kuei ch'uan,*[2] Chap. 32, "On chanting"), the name Mâtṛceta is mentioned, but I-tsing does not identify him with Açvaghosha, though the legend attached to the former closely resembles that of the latter told in Târanâtha. Târanâtha states that when Açvaghosha became a sthavira and advocate of the

---

[1] *Geschichte des Buddhismus*, p. 90.

[2] 南海寄歸傳 by I-tsing 義淨 who left China A. D. 671 for a pilgrimage to India and came back A. D. 695. The book is a work on the vinaya as observed by the Sarvâstivâdin, which the pilgrim witnessed in India as well as in Ceylon. An English transtion by J. Takakusu, London.

Tripitaka, he had a dream one night in which the venerable Târâ gave him the instruction to write hymns on Buddha for the expiation of his former sinful deeds ; that according to this admonition he wrote many hymns praising the virtues of Buddha, amongst which one containing one hundred and fifty çlokas[1] is the best of all ; that the hymns composed by him are full of benediction like the very words of Buddha, because he was predicted by the Blessed One to be a hymnist.[2]

Compare the above with this from I-tsing :

"The venerable Mâtṛceṭa (Mother-child) was a man of great intellect, of excellent virtue, eminently standing above all sages in India. A tradition says that when Buddha was taking a walk one time with his kinsmen, disciples, and many other people, a nightingale (?), observing his personal feature as elegant and majestic as a gold mountain, uttered in the wood some pleasant, harmonious notes that sounded like praising the virtues of Buddha. Buddha then turning towards the disciples said : 'The bird overcome by the joy of seeing me utters a pitiful cry. By this merit it will after my death obtain a human form, Mâtṛceṭa 摩呾哩制吒 by name, and praise and adore my intrinsic virtues with a number of hymns.' This man first followed the doctrine of a tîrthaka worshipping Maheç-

---

[1] Schiefner notes : Çatapantschâçatika nâma stotra, **Tandjur** B. 1, unter den Stotra's.

[2] *Geschichte des Buddhismus*, p. 91.

vara[1] and composed many hymns to adore him. But
in the meantime he came across his own name recorded
[in a Buddhist writing]; inspired by this, he took refuge in Buddha, changed his garb, abandoned his
laymanship, and in many ways praised, honored and
adored Buddha. Regretting his misbehavior in the
past and desiring to perform good deeds in the future
and also lamenting the unfortunate fate that prevented
him from having a personal interview with the Great
Teacher rather than bowing before his bequeathed
image, he at last decided with all his rhetorical talent
and in solemn fulfilment of the Lord's prophecy, to
praise his virtues and merits [in hymns]. He first
composed four hundred çlokas and then one hundred
and fifty çlokas;[2] all of which describe the six Pâramitâs [Perfections] and state the excellent virtues
possessed by the World-Honored-One," etc.

At the end of the same Chapter (i. e., Chap. 32)
in I-tsing's *Correspondence* he refers to Açvaghosha and
Nagârjuna both of whom composed some beautiful
and popular hymns that were sung by Buddhists
throughout India at the time of his pilgrimage. But if
the Tibetan statement is reliable, I-tsing may have

[1] Cf. the following statement in Târanâtha, p. 90: "Als er
(Açvaghosha) in den Mantra- und Tantra-Formeln und in der Dia-
lektik sehr bewandert wurde, gab ihm Maheçvara selbst Anlei-
tung."

[2] "Hymn of One Hundred and Fifty Çlokas" (Çatapañcâshad-
buddhastotra), translated into Chinese by I-tsing during his stay in
the Nâlanda-vihâra, Central India. At the time of the compilation
of the *Chêng yüan catalogue* the original is said to have existed.

been mistaken in recording Açvaghosha and Mâtrceṭa as different characters. The Tibetan and Chinese version of the one hundred and fifty çloka hymn being still existent, the comparison of which, however, I have not yet been able to make, will furnish an interesting testimony for the identification.

Many legendary explanations have been invented about the name of Açvaghosha, as might be expected of the imaginative Indian mind, but not being worth while quoting from the materials at my command, no reference will be made to them here.

CONVERSIONS.

A consensus of traditions both Tibetan and Chinese maintains that Açvaghosha was in his earlier life a most powerful adherent of Brahmanism, though we are tempted to discredit it on the ground that later Buddhist writers may have wished to exaggerate the superiority of Buddhism to all other Indian philosophical and religious doctrines, by chronicling the conversion of one of its strongest opponents to their side. Whatever the origin of the legend may be, how did his conversion take place? By whom was he converted? About these points the Tibetan and the Chinese tradition by no means agree, the one standing in a direct contradiction to the other. While the Tibetan account is full of mystery and irrationality, the Chinese is natural enough to convince us of its probable occurrence.

According to Târanâtha[1] Âryadeva, the most eminent disciple of Nâgârjuna, defeated and proselyted Açvaghosha,[2] not by his usual subtlety in dialectics, but by the superiority of his magical arts. Açvaghosha made use of every tantric formula he could command, in order to free himself from the enchantment in which he was held by his enemy, but all to no purpose whatever. Thus when he was in an utterly desperate condition, he happened to read the Buddhist Sûtra which was kept in his place of confinement and in which he found his destiny prophesied by Buddha,[3] he was seized with deep regret for his former hostile attitude toward the Dharma, and immediately renouncing his tîrthakism, professed the doctrine of Çâkyamuni.

The Tibetan tradition presents some unmistakable indications of a later invention: the use of tantric formulæ, the so-called prophecy of the Tathâgata, and the anachronism of Âryadeva. On the other hand, the Chinese records are worth crediting, though they are not unanimous as to how the conversion took place and who was the proselytist.

According to the *Life of Açvaghosha*, Parçva[4] was

[1] *Geschichte des Buddhismus*, German translation by Schiefner, pp. 84–85.

[2] He is mentioned there by the name of Durdarshakâla.

[3] Cf. this with the accounts of Mâtrceta-Açvaghosha told in I-tsing.

[4] The conversion of Açvaghosha by Parçva as here stated may be considered an addition to the proof already demonstrated for the contemporaneousness of Açvaghosha and King Kanishka; for

the man who converted him. They agreed at their
first meeting that on the seventh day thence they
should have the king, ministers, çrâmanas, tîrthakas
and all great teachers of the Dharma gathered in the
Vihâra and have their discussion there before all those
people. ''In the sixth night the sthavira entered into
a samâdhi and meditated on what he had to do [in
the morning]. When the seventh day dawned, a great
crowd was gathered like clouds. The Sthavira Parçva
arrived first and ascended a high platform with an
unusually pleasant countenance. The tîrthaka [i. e.,
Açvaghosha] came later and took a seat opposite
him. When he observed the çrâmana with a pleasant
countenance and in good spirits, and when he also
observed his whole attitude showing the manner of
an able opponent, he thought: 'May he not be Bhikshu Chin? His mind is calm and pleasant, and besides he bears the manner of an able antagonist. We
shall indeed have an excellent discussion to-day.'

''They then proposed the question how the defeated one should be punished. The tîrthaka [Açva-
ghosha] said: 'The defeated one shall have his tongue
cut out.' The sthavira replied: 'No, he shall become
a disciple [of the winner] as the acknowledgement of
defeat.' The tîrthaka then replied: 'Let it be so,'
and asked, 'Who will begin the discussion?' The

Parçva, according to the Tibetan as well as the Chinese authority,
was a co-operator at least, if not the president, of the third Buddhist convocation promoted by the King of Kashmir.

Sthavira Parçva said: 'I am more advanced in age; I came from afar for the purpose [of challenging you]; and moreover I was here this morning earlier than you. So it will be most natural for me to speak first.' The tîrthaka said: 'Let it be so. Following the subject of your argument, I shall completely baffle you.'

"The Sthavira Parçva then said: 'What shall we have to do, in order to keep the kingdom in perfect peace, to have the king live long, to let the people enjoy abundance and prosperity, all free from evils and catastrophies?' The tîrthaka was silent, not knowing what to reply. As now according to the rule of discussion one who could not make a response is defeated, Açvaghosha was obliged to bow [before the opponent] as a disciple of his. He had his head shaved, was converted to a çrâmana, and instructed in the perfection-precepts.

"When he [Açvaghosha] was alone in his room, he was absorbed in gloomy, unpleasant reflexion as to why he, possessing a bright intellect and far-sighted discretion, and having his reputation widely spread all over the world, could be defeated with a single question and be made a disciple of another. Parçva well knew his mind and ordered him to come to his room where the master manifested himself in several supernatural transformations. Açvaghosha now fully recognised that his master was not a man of ordinary type, and thus feeling happy and contented, thought it his duty to become one of his disciples.

"The master told him: 'Your intellect is bright enough, hard to find its equal; but it wants a final touch. If you study the doctrine I have mastered, attend to my capability and insight into the Bodhi, and if you become thoroughly versed in the method of discussion and clearly understand the principle of things, there will be no one who can match you in the whole world.'

"The master returned to his own country [North India]; the disciple remained in Central India, making an extensive study of the Sûtras, seeking a clear comprehension of the doctrine, Buddhistic as well as non-Buddhistic. His oratorical genius swept everything before him, and he was reverentially honored by the four classes of the people, including the king of [Central] India who treated him as a man of distinction."

According to the *Transmission of the Dharmapitaka* (*Fu fa tsang chuan*), however, Açvaghosha was not converted by Parçva, but by his disciple and patriarchal successor, Puṇyayaças. Though the two works, *Life of Açvaghosha* and the book just mentioned, differ in some other points, they are evidently two different versions of the one original legend. As the book is not as yet accessible to English readers, I here produce the whole matter translated from the Chinese version. The comparison will prove interesting.

"Full of a proud and arrogant spirit that speedily grew like a wild plant, he [Açvaghosha] firmly believed in the existence of an ego-entity and cherished the ultra-egotistic idea. Being informed that an Âcarya called Puṇyayaças, who, deep in knowledge and wide in learning, proclaimed that all things are relative [=çûnya, lit. empty], there is no ātman, no budgala; Açvaghosha's arrogant spirit asserted itself, and presenting himself to Puṇyayaças challenged him saying: 'I confute all [false] opinions and doctrines in the world, as hailstones strike tender grass. If my declaration prove false and not true, I will have my own tongue cut out in acknowledgment of defeat.' Thereupon Puṇyayaças explained to him that Buddhism distinguishes two kinds of truth, that while 'practical truth' hypothetically admits the existence of an ātman, there is nothing conditional in 'pure [or absolute] truth,' all being calm and tranquil, and that therefore we cannot prove the ego as an absolute entity.

"Açvaghosha would not yet surrender himself, because being over-confident of his own intellectual power he considered himself to have gained the point. Puṇyayaças said: 'Carefully think of yourself; tell not a lie. We will see which of us has really won.'

"Açvaghosha meanwhile came to think that while 'practical truth' being only conditional has no reality at all, 'pure truth' is calm and tranquil in its nature, and that therefore these two forms of truth are all unobtainable, and that if they have thus no actuality [or existence], how could they be refuted [as false]? So feeling now the superiority of his opponent, he tried to cut out his tongue in acknowledgement of the defeat. But Puṇyayaças stopped him, saying : 'We teach a doctrine of love and compassion, and do not demand that you cut out your tongue. Have your head shaved instead and be my disciple.' Açvaghosha thus converted was made a çrâmana by Puṇyayaças.

"But Açvaghosha who felt extremely ashamed of his [former] self-assumption was thinking of attempting his own life. Puṇyayaças, however, attaining arhatship, entered into a samâdhi and divined what was going on in the mind of Açvaghosha. He ordered him to go and bring some books out of the library. Açvaghosha said to the Âcarya: 'The room is perfectly dark; how can I get in there?' To this Puṇya-yaças answered : 'Just go in, and I shall let you have light.' Then the Âcarya through his supernatural power stretched far into the room his right hand whose five fingers each radiating with light illuminated everything inside of the walls. Açvaghosha thought it a mental hallucination, and knowing the fact that a hallucination as a rule disappears when one is conscious of it, he was surprised to see the

¹ The reasoning is somewhat unintelligible. The passages must be defective, and although I might venture to supply the necessary words to make them more logical and intelligible to the general reader who is not acquainted with the çûnyatâ philosophy. I have not tried to do so, thinking that it is enough here if we see in what the subject of the discussion consisted.

light glowing more and more. He tried his magical arts to extinguish it till he felt utterly exhausted, for the mysterious light suffered no change whatever. Finally coming to realise that it was the work of no other person than his teacher, his spirit was filled with remorse, and he thenceforth applied himself diligently to religious discipline and never relapsed."[1]

The *Record of Buddha and the Patriarchs* (*Fo tsou tung tsai*) agrees with the *Transmission of the Dharmapitaka* (*Fu fa tsang chuan*) in making Puṇyayaças, instead of Parçva, the master of the conversion. But the former does not state how Açvaghosha was converted.

Though so far it remains an open question who was the real master of Açvaghosha, we can be sure of this, that he had intimate spiritual communication with both Parçva and Puṇyayaças. Parçva, who was an older contemporary of Puṇyayaças, was probably already advanced in age when Açvaghosha came to be personally acquainted with him, and so he did not have time enough to lead the young promising disciple to a consummate understanding of the doctrine of Buddha. After the demise of this venerable old patriarch, Açvaghosha therefore had to go to Puṇya-yaças for a further study of his religion, till he was capable of forming his own original thoughts, which are set forth in his principal work, the *Discourse of*

[1] The *Transmission of the Dharmapitaka* (*Fu fa tsang chuan*) *fas.* 5.

the Awakening of Faith (Çraddhotpâda-çastra). This
assumption is justified when we notice that Açvaghosha in the *Book of Great Glory* pays his homage to
Parçva as well as to Puṇyayaças.

Now by way of a supplementary note to the above,
let us say a word about Wassiljew's observation,[1]
which states that while Hînayânists or Çrâvakas ascribe the conversion of Açvaghosha to Parçva, the
Mahâyânistic record says that Âryadeva converted
him. This assertion is evidently incorrect, for the
Life of Açvaghosha as well as the *Transmission of the
Dharmapitaka (Fu fa tsang chuan)* in which the honor
of his conversion is given to the successor of Parçva
as aforesaid, do not certainly belong to the work of
the Hînayâna school. It is the Tibetan tradition only,
and not the general Mahâyânist statement, that Âryadeva converted Açvaghosha, and there is no ground
at all for the assertion of Wassiljew, which practically
leads us to take everything Tibetan for Mahâyânistic
and everything Chinese for Hînayânistic.

LISTS OF PATRIARCHS.

The incorrectness of the Tibetan story, as to the
conversion of Açvaghosha by Âryadeva above referred
to, is further shown by a list of the Buddhist patriarchs in India appearing in various Buddhist books
either translated from Sanskrit into Chinese or com-

[1] *Buddhismus*, German edition, p. 222, and also see Târanâtha, translated by Schiefner, p. 311.

piled in China from sundry sources. In every one of them Açvaghosha is placed after Parçva or Puṇya-

SARVASTI-VADIN	BUDDHABHADRA[1]	THE FU FA TSANG CHUAN	THE FO TSU T'UNG CHI	THE FO TSU T'UNG TSAI	No.
Mahâkâçyapa		Mahâkâçyapa	Mahâkâçyapa	Mahâkâçyapa	1
Ânanda	Ânanda	Ânanda	Ânanda	Ânanda	2
Madhyântika	Madhyântika	Çanavâsa	Çanavâsa	Çanavâsa	3
Çanavâsa	Çanavâsa	Upagupta	Upagupta	Upagupta	4
Upagupta	Upagupta	Drtaka	Drtaka	Drtaka	5
Maitreya	Kâtyâyana	Micchaka	Micchaka	Micchaka	6
Kâtyâyana	Vasumitra	Buddhananndi	Buddhanandi	Vasumitra	7
Vasumitra	Krshna	Buddhamitra	Buddhamitra	Buddhânandi	8
Krshna	Parçva	Parçva	Parçva	Buddhamitra	9
Parçva	Açvaghosha	Punyayaças	Punyayaças	Parçva	10
Açvaghosha	Ghosha	Açvaghosha	Açvaghosha	Punyayaças	11
Kumârata		Kapimala	Kapi	Açvaghosha	12
		Nâgârjuna	Nâgârjuna	Kapimala	13
			Kanadeva	Nâgârjuna	14
				Kanadeva (Âryadeva)	15
Nâgârjuna					34
Deva					35

[1] He was a native of Kapilavastu and came to China A D. 406. A translator of many Sanskrit works. His list belongs to the Sarvâstivâdin, though it is a little different from the succeeding one. The former contains fifty-four and the latter fifty-three patriarchs. See the *Ch'u san tsang chi chi* 出三藏記集 by 僧祐 (Nanjo's Catalogue, No. 1476).

yaças, and before both Nâgârjuna and Âryadeva, the most brilliant disciple of the former. The list on the opposite page, therefore, as noticed elsewhere, will furnish good material for fixing the time of Açvaghosha. It does not make any practical difference whether he was converted by Parçva himself or his immediate successor and disciple Puṇyayaças, because it is most probable they all were contemporaneous. The list generally gives twenty-three or twenty-eight patriarchs beginning with Mahâkâçyapa, but not deeming it necessary to give a complete list, I have cut it short at Deva.

Chieh-sung[1] refutes in his *Chuan fa chang tsung lun* 傳法正宗論 (*A Treatise on the Right Transmission of the Dharma*) the authority of the *Transmission of the Dharmapitaka* (*Fu fa tsang chuan*), but he agrees with it down to the seventeenth patriarch. The principal point of his refutation is simply that Bodhidharma, the founder of the Chinese Dhyâna school, should be included in the list.

AS AN ARTIST.

We cannot conclude the accounts concerning Açvaghosha without mentioning an anecdote from a Chinese source.[2] The *Çraddhotpâdaçâstra* (*The Awak-*

---

[1] 智昇, a priest of the Dhyâna school who died A. D. 1071 or 1072. He wrote among other works one on the fundamental identicalness of Confucianism and Buddhism.

[2] The *Transmission of the Dharmapitaka* (*Fu fa tsang chuan, fas.* 5).

ening of Faith,) proves he was a philosopher of a high
grade; the *Buddhacaritakâvya* (*The Life of Buddha*)
and the *Mahâlamkâraçâstra* (*The Book of Great Glory*)
reveal his poetical genius; and the following story in-
dicates that he was a musician : [1]

"He [Açvaghosha] then went to Pâtaliputra for
his propaganda-tour, where he composed an excellent
tune called Lai cha huo lo (嬾吒和囉 *Râstavara?*),
that he might by this means convert the people of the
city. Its melody was classical, mournful, and melodious, inducing the audience to ponder on the misery,
emptiness, and non-âtman-ness of life. That is to say,
the music roused in the mind of the hearer the thought
that all aggregates are visionary and subject to transformation; that the triple world is a jail and a bondage, with nothing enjoyable in it; that since royalty,
nobility, and the exercise of supreme power, are all
characterised with transitoriness, nothing can prevent
their decline, which will be as sure as the dispersion
of the clouds in the sky; that this corporeal existence
is a sham, is as hollow as a plantain tree, is an enemy,
a foe, one not to be intimately related with; and again
that like a box in which a cobra is kept, it should

[1] The fact agrees well with Târanâtha's statement which in its
German translation reads as follows: "Die von ihm verfassten
Loblieder sind auch in allen Ländern verbreitet; da zuletzt Sän-
ger und Possenreisser dieselben vortrugen und bei allen Menschen
des Landes mit Macht Glauben an den Buddha entstand, erwuchs
durch die Loblieder grösserer Nutzen zur Verbreitung der Lehre."
Geschichte des Buddhismus, German translation, p. 91.

never be cherished by anybody; that therefore all
Buddhas denounce persons clinging to a corporeal
existence. Thus explaining in detail the doctrine of
the non-âtman and the *çûnyatâ*, Açvaghosha had the
melody played by musicians, who, however, not being
able to grasp the significance of the piece, failed to
produce the intended tune and harmony. He then
donned a white woolen dress, joined the band of musicians, beating the drum, ringing the bell, and tuning
the lyre, and this done, the melody in full perfection
gave a note at once mournful and soothing, so as to
arouse in the mind of the audience the idea of the
misery, emptiness, and non-âtman-ness of all things.
The five hundred royal princes in the city thus moved
all at once were fully awakened, and abhorring the
curse of the five evil passions abandoned their worldly
life and took refuge in the Bodhi. The king of Pâtaliputra was very much terrified by the event, thinking
that if the people who listen to this music would
abandon their homes [like the princes], his country
would be depopulated and his royal business ruined.
So he warned the people never to play this music
hereafter.

WORKS IN CHINESE TRANSLATIONS.

The works ascribed to Açvaghosha and still existing in Chinese translations are eight in number. They
are: (1) The 大乘起信論 *Tai shêng ch'i hsin lun* (*Mahâyânaçraddhotpâdaçâstra*): *discourse on the awakening of*

faith in the Mahâyâna. It is the principal work of
Açvaghosha, and through this we are able to recognise
what an important position he occupies in the development of the Mahâyânistic world-conception and theory of final emancipation. Its outlines and the accounts of its Chinese translation will be given below.
(2) The 大宗地玄文本論 *Ta sung ti hsüan wên pên lun,*
a fundamental treatise on the spiritual stages for reaching
final deliverance. The book has a decided tendency to
mysticism, explaining a gradual development of religious consciousness through fifty-one different spiritual stages. It may be considered a precursory work
out of which Vajrabodhi's Mantrism finally made a
full manifestation. It was translated by Paramârtha
between A. D. 557–569. Twenty *fasciculi,* forty chapters. (3) The 大莊嚴論經 *Ta chuang yen lun ching*
(*Mahâlamkârasûtraçâstra*), the *Book of Great Glory,* or
a compilation of stories illustrating the retribution of
karma. The stories relate mostly to the events that
occurred in Western India. Beal translated some of
them in his *Buddhist Literature in China.* The Chinese
translator is Kumârajîva, *circa* A. D. 405. Fifteen
fasciculi. (4) The 佛所行讚 *Fo shu hing tsan* (*Buddha-*
caritakâvya), a well known poem on the life of Buddha.
The Chinese translation is by Dharmaraksha between
A. D. 414-421. Five *fasciculi,* twenty eight chapters,
Beal's English translation forms Vol. XIX. of *The*
Sacred Books of the East; and Cowell's translation from
Sanskrit, Vol. XLIX of the same. (5) The 尼乾子

問 無 我 義 經 *Ni kan tzŭ wên wu wu i ching, a sûtra on
a Nirgrantha's asking about the theory of non-ego.* The
book foreshadows the Mâdhyamika philosophy of
Nâgârjuna, for the two forms of truth are distinguished
there, Pure Truth (*Parmârtha-satya*) and Practical
Truth (*Samvrtti-satya*),[1] and the *Çûnyatâ* theory also is
proclaimed. (6) The 十不善業道經 *Shih pu shan yeh tao
ching, a sûtra on the ten no-good deeds.* (7) The 事師法五
十頌 *Shih shih fa wu shih sung,* fifty verses on the rules
of serving a master or teacher. (8) The 六趣輪廻經
*Lu tao lun 'hui ching, a sûtra on transmigration through
the six states of existence.* These last four works are
very short, all translated by Jih-ch'êng (Divayaças?),
between A. D. 1004–1058.

CHINESE TRANSLATIONS OF THE "DISCOURSE ON THE AWAKENING OF FAITH."

Let us give here some remarks on the Chinese
translations of Açvaghosha's principal and best known
work *The Awakening of Faith.* The Sanskrit original
is long lost, probably owing to the repeated persecu-
tions of Buddhism by Chinese emperors at different
times. According to the *Chéng yüan catalogue* 貞元錄
(compiled between A. D. 785–804) the Sanskrit text
is said to have existed at that time. It is a great pity
that such an important Buddhist philosophical work

---

[1] Notice Açvaghosha's discussion with Puṇyayaças as above
mentioned.

as the present çâstra can be studied only through translations.[1]

There are two Chinese translations still existing in the Tripiṭaka collection. The first translation was made by Paramârtha (波羅末陀), otherwise called Kulanâtha (狗羅那陀), of Ujjayana (or Ujjayini, modern Oujein) in Western India. He came to China A. D. 546 and died A. D. 569 when he was 71 years old. Among many other translations, the present one came from his pen on the tenth day of September, A. D. 554.

The second one is by Çikshânanda (實叉難陀), of Kusutana (Khoten), who began his work on the eighth of October, A. D. 700. He died in China A. D. 710 at the age of 59.

As to the problem whether the original of the two Chinese translations is the same or different, my impression is that they were not the same text, the one having been brought from Ujjayana and the other from Khoten. But the difference, as far as we can judge from the comparison of the two versions, is not fundamental.

In the preface to the second translation of the Kao

[1] An inquiry has been made by the present English translator as to whether the original Sanskrit copy could be found either in India or in Nepal; but Prof. Satis Chandra Âchâryya, of the Buddhist Text Society, Calcutta, with whom he has been communicating on the subject, informs him that as far as India is concerned there is almost no hope of securing it, and also that his friend in Nepal has been unable so far to discover the original,

li edition, the unknown writer states to the following effect: "The present Çâstra has two translations. The first one is by Paramârtha and the second one is from the Sanskrit text brought by Çikshânanda who found also the older Sanskrit original in the Tz'u an tower. As soon as he had finished the rendering of the Avatamsakasûtra into Chinese, he began a translation of his own text with the assistance of several native Buddhist priests. The new translation occasionally deviates from the older one, partly because each translator had his own views and partly because the texts themselves were not the same."

Though the *Chéng yüan* 貞元錄 as well as the *K'ai yüan*[1] 開元錄 catalogue affirm that the two translations were from the same text, this can only mean that they were not radically divergent. For if any two editions differ so slightly as not to affect the essential points, they can be said to be practically the same text.

Which of the two translations then is the more correct? To this question we cannot give any definite answer as the originals are missing. The first translation has found a more popular acceptance in Japan as well as in China, not because it is more faithful to the original, but because a most learned and illustrious Buddhist scholar called Fa tsang 法藏 (A. D.

---

[1] A catalogue of Buddhist books collected in the K'ai yüan period (A. D. 713–741) of the Tung Dynasty, by 契嵩 Chih-shang, A. D. 730. Its full name *K'ai yüan shih chiao lu.* Twenty *fasciculi.*

643–712) wrote a commentary on it. And on that account the commentary is more studied than the text itself. Fa tsang assisted Çikshânanda in preparing the second translation, but he preferred the first one for his commentary work, partly because the first one had already found a wide circulation and some commentators before his time, and partly because both translations agreeing in all their important points, he did not like to show his "partiality," as a commentator on Fa tsang says, to the one in the preparation of which he himself took part.

The present English translation is made from the second Chinese version by Çikshânanda, but the first version has been carefully compared with it, and wherever disagreements occur between them they have been noticed in footnotes.

OUTLINES OF THE "DISCOURSE ON THE AWAKENING OF FAITH."

I cannot help saying a few words here about the importance of Açvaghosha's main work which is scarcely known in the West, and if so, wrongly. Even Samuel Beal who is considered one of the best authorities on Chinese Buddhism, makes a misleading reference to our author in his *Buddhism in China*. The following quotation from the same apparently shows that at least when he wrote it, in 1884, he had a very insufficient knowledge of the subject. He says (page 138):

"His (Açvaghosha's) writings still survive in a Chinese form, and when examined will probably be found to be much tinged by a pseudo-Christian element. . . . But there is one book, the *K'i-sin-lun*, or 'Treatise for Awakening Faith,' which has never yet been properly examined, but, so far as is known, is based on doctrines foreign to Buddhism and allied to a perverted form of Christian dogma." The incorrectness of this statement will readily be seen by the reader when we proceed further on.

Wassiljew, another of the highest Western authorities on the subject, seems to be entirely ignorant of the existence of the present work. It is very strange that those who are considered to be quite well acquainted with the development of the Mahâyânistic thought, do not place in the right light a prominent, if not the principal, actor, who, so far as is known to us, practically initiated this great spiritual and intellectual movement in India. Wassiljew says in his *Buddhismus* (pp. 83–84):

"Zu welcher besonderen Schule Açvaghosha gehörte, wird nicht mit Bestimmtheit überliefert: aus der Legende, nach welcher er sich bei der Abfassung der Vibhâshâ betheiligte, dürfen wir jedoch den Schluss ziehen, dass er zu den Repräsentanten der Vaibhâschika's gerechnet ward."

It is true that in the *Life of Vasubandhu* Açvaghosha is said to have taken part in the compilation of the Vibhâshâ, but it is of no account whatever in the face of the present book in which we can clearly trace almost all elements of the thought fully developed afterwards by Nâgârjuna and other later Mahâyâna representatives.

I wish here, in order to show the significance of Açvaghosha, to call the attention of the reader to the three most salient points in his doctrine which will distinguish him from all Hînayâna schools. The three points constituting the gist of this Çâstra then are: (1) the conception of suchness (*Bhûtatathatâ*); (2) the theory of the triple personality; (3) the salvation by faith or the Sukhâvati doctrine.

The conception of suchness assumes other names, namely, The Womb of the Tathâgata (*Thatâgata-garbha*), when considered from its embracing all possible merits, and the All-Conserving Mind (*Âlaya-vijñâna*), when it becomes the principle of evolution and is said to have developed from the teaching of Buddha as expounded in the old canonical sûtras, such as the *Lankâvatara* and the *Çrîmâlâ*. Whatever the origin of the idea of suchness might have been, its "absolute aspect" evidently foreshadows the *Çûnyatâ* philosophy of the Mâdhyamika school. It is very doubtful whether Nâgârjuna, as told in a Chinese tradition, was a personal disciple of Açvaghosha, but it is highly probable that he was much influenced by him in forming his system.

The second thesis, the theory of the triple personality, that is one of the most distinctive characteris-

tics of the Mahâyâna Buddhism, seems to have been
first established by Açvaghosha. The pantheistic idea
of suchness (*Bhûtatathatâ*), and the religious consciousness which always tends to demand something
embodied in infinite love (*karunâ*) and infinite wisdom
(*jñâna*), and the scientific conception of the law of
causation regulating our ethical as well as physical
world, or in short the doctrine of karma,—these three
factors working together in the mind of Açvaghosha,
culminated in his theory of the triple personality.

The doctrine of salvation by faith whereon the
Japanese Shin Shyû (True Sect) and Jôdô Shyû (Pure
Land Sect) laid down their foundation also, appears
first in the present çâstra.   If the quotation in the
Mahâyânaçraddhotpâda actually refers to the Sukhhâ-
vatî Sûtras, as we may fairly assume, there is a great
probability in the statement that during the first four
centuries after the Nirvâna there was already a variety
of free interpretations about the teaching of the Master, which, commingled with the other religio-philo-
sophical thoughts in India, eventually made a full development under the generel names of the Mahâyâna
and the Hînayâna schools.

A supplementary point to be noticed in Açvaghosha is the abundance of similar thoughts and passages
with those in the *Bhagavadgîta*.   The coincidence between the latter and the *Saddharmapuṇḍarîka* has been
pointed out by Kern in his *Buddhismus und seine Geschichte* (Vol. II., p. 500, footnote).   While it is an

open question which of the two has an earlier date, the Mahâyâna Buddhism as a whole must be permitted to have some common points with the canonical book of Çivaism.

In conclusion I wish to state that as this book, the *Awakening of Faith*, is of paramount importance in its being the first attempt of systematising the fundamental thoughts of the Mahâyâna Buddhism, as well as in its forming a main authority of all the Mahâyânistic schools, those who study the doctrinal history of Buddhism cannot dispense with it; and that, in spite of its highest importance, no attempt has yet been made to make it accessible to the reader who is not familiar with the Chinese language, and so I here offer to the public an English translation of the entire text.

ADORATION.

ADORATION to the World-honored Ones (*Bhaga-vat*)[1] in all the ten quarters, who universally produce great benefits, whose wisdom is infinite and transcendent, and who save and guard [all beings].

[Adoration] to the Dharma[2] whose essence and

---

[1] There are ten appellations most commonly given to a Buddha: (1) *Tathâgata* (the one who thus comes, or he who has been expected and fulfils all expectations, the perfect one); (2) *Arhat* (the worthy one, but according to Nâgârjuna's *Mahâprajnâpâramitâçâstra*, Chinese translation by Kumârajîva, Vol. III., p. 17, one who has destroyed all enemies of evil passions, or one who is revered by gods and men, or one who will not be reborn; see also Vol. II., p. 20); (3) *Samyaksambuddha* (one who is perfect by enlightenment); (4) *Vidyâcaranasampanna* (one who is perfect in knowledge and conduct); (5) *Sugata* (one who goes well); (6) *Lokavid* (one who knows the world); (7) *Anuttara* (one who has no superior); (8) *Purushadamyasârathi* (the tamer of all beings); (9) *Câstâdevâmanushyânâm* (the teacher of gods and men); (10) *Buddha* (the enlightened one). When *Lokavid* and *Anuttara* are considered to be one title, as in the *Sutra on the Ten Apellations*, *Bhagavat* is added to make the tenth.

[2] According to a general interpretation of Mahâyâna Buddhists dharma means: (1) that which exists; (2) the object of understanding. Dharma may therefore be rendered in the first sense by "object," or "thing," or "substance," or "being," including everything mental as well as physical in its broadest sense, and so sarvadharma will designate all possible existences in the uni-

attributes are like the ocean, revealing to us the principle of anâtman and forming the storage of infinite merits.

[Adoration] to the congregation (*samgha*) of those who assiduously aspire after perfect knowledge (*samvaksambodhi*).

That all beings (*sarvasattva*) may rid themselves of doubt, become free from evil attachment, and, by the awakening of faith (*çraddha*), inherit Buddhaseeds, I write this Discourse.[1]

verse; while dharma in the second sense may safely be rendered by "law" or "doctrine" as generally understood by Western Buddhist scholars, to most of whom, however, the first significance of the term is strangely unknown. Max Müller fitly remarks in his introduction to the English translation of the *Vajracchedîkâ*, p. xiv: "Dharma in its ordinary Buddhist phraseology may be correctly rendered by law. Thus the whole teaching of Buddha is called the good law, Saddharma. But in our treatise dharma is generally used in a different sense. It means form (εἶδος) and likewise what is possessed of form, what is therefore different from other things, what is individual, in fact, what we mean by a thing or an object. This meaning has escaped most of the translators, both Oriental and Western, but if we were always to translate dharma by law, it seems to me that the whole drift of our treatise would become unintelligible." In this translation dharma is rendered sometimes by "thing," sometimes by "law," sometimes by "truth" or "doctrine," according to the context. But when it is synonymous with suchness (*bhûtatathatâ*), I have retained its original Sanskrit form, capitalised.

[1]An almost similar passage is repeated in the succeeding paragraph, while it does not occur in the older translation It may be a mistake on the part of the new translation, but I have left it as it stands in the text.

DISCOURSE.

FOR the purpose of awakening in all beings a pure faith in the Mahâyâna,[1] of destroying their doubts and attachment to false doctrines, and of affording them an uninterrupted inheritance of Buddha-seeds, I write this Discourse.

There is a principle whereby the root of faith in the Mahâyâna can be produced, and I shall explain it.

The explanation consists of five parts:

[1] The term Mahâyâna here seems not to have been used as it usually is in contrast to the Hînayâna. Açvaghosha adopts it simply to denote the greatness of suchness (*bhûtatathatâ*) as well as to prove its being the safest and surest means of salvation. It is therefore the name given to the first principle itself, and not to any philosophical system or religious dogmatics. But the term used in this wise by Açvaghosha and perhaps in earlier Mahâyâna texts gradually lost its original sense in the course of the development of this progressive religious view. It was then transferred to distinguish the system at large from that of the so-called Çrâvakas, to which the followers of the former gave in contrast to their own the rather humiliating name Hînayâna. At the time of Açvaghosha the controversy between them was probably not as vehement as it proved later on. And this fact may be seen from the tolerant spirit shown in the third convocation under the reign of King Kanishka. By the Mahâyâna followers Açvaghosha is unanimously recognised as the forerunner of Nâgârjuna by whose marvellous genius the system was brought to maturity.

I. Introductory.

II. General Statement of Principles.

III. The Explanation Itself.

IV. The Practice of Faith.

V. Benefits [derived therefrom].

I. INTRODUCTORY.

There are eight inducements [to write this Discourse]:

1. A general object, i. e., that the author might induce all beings to liberate themselves from misery and to enjoy blessing, and not that he might gain thereby some worldly advantages, etc.

2. That he might unfold the fundamental truth of the Tathâgata and let all beings have a right comprehension of it.

3. That he might enable those who have brought their root of merit (*kuçalamûla*) to maturity and obtained immovable faith, to have a philosophical grasp of the doctrine of the Mahâyâna.

4. That he might enable those whose root of merit is weak and insignificant, to acquire faith and to advance to the stage of immovable firmness (*avaivarti-katva*).[1]

5. That he might induce all beings to obliterate

---

[1] *Avaivartikatva* means literally "never retreat." Faith is said to become immovably firm when one enters into the group of those who cannot be shaken in the possession of absolute truth (*samyaktvaniyataraçi*). For a further explanation see the reference in the Index to *samyaktvaniyataraçi*.

the previously acquired evils (*durgati* or *karmâvarana*), to restrain their own thoughts, and to free themselves from the three venomous passions.[1]

6. That he might induce all beings to practise the orthodox method of cessation [or tranquilisation *çamatha*] and of intellectual insight (*vidarçana*),[2] to be fortified against the commission of mental trespasses due to inferiority of mind.

7. That he might induce all beings in the right way to ponder on the doctrine of the Mahâyâna, for thus they will be born in the presence of Buddhas,[3] and acquire the absolutely immovable Mahâyâna-faith.

8. That he might, by disclosing those benefits which are produced by joyfully believing in the Mahâyâna, let sentient beings become acquainted with the final aim of their efforts.

Though all these doctrines are sufficiently set forth

---

[1] They are: (1) covetousness (*lobha*); (2) malice (*dvesha*); (3) ignorance (*moha*).

[2] *Camatha* and *Vidarçana* or *Vipaçyana* constitute one of the five methods of discipline, for whose full explanation see the reference in the Index to these terms.

[3] This passage, which is considered to be a reference to the Sukhâvatî Sûtras, such as the Larger and the Smaller *Sukhâvatî-vyûha*, or the *Amitâyur-dhyâna*, seems to prove that some of the Mahâyâna texts of the Pure Land Sect had been in existence before the time of Açvaghosha who gives towards the end of his Discourse a quotation apparently taken from one of the above-mentioned Sûtras. The Sûtras therefore must be at least one or two hundred years older than Açvaghosha, in order that they might be quoted as an authentic teaching of Buddha.

in the Mahâyâna Sûtras,[1] yet as the predispositions and inclinations of the people[2] are not the same, and the conditions for obtaining enlightenment vary, I now write this Discourse.

There is another reason for doing so. At the time of the Tathâgata the people were unusually gifted, and the Buddha's presence, majestic both in mind and body, served to unfold the infinite significances of the Dharma with simplicity and yet in perfection. Accordingly there was no need for a philosophical discourse (çâstra).

After the Nirvâna of the Buddha there were men who possessed in themselves the intellectual power to understand the many-sided meanings of the Sûtras,[3]

---

[1] The view here proposed by Açvaghosha, which is called by Chinese Buddhists the theory of the evolution of the Tathâgata-garbha, is considered to be an elucidation of the doctrine taught by Buddha in such Mahâyâna Sûtras as the *Lankâvatâra*, *Ghana-vyûha*, *Crîmâlâ*, etc.

[2] Literally, those who are to be converted.

[3] There are twelve divisions called *Angas* in the Mahâyânist writings, while in the Pâli only nine are counted. The twelve *angas* are: (1) *sûtra* (aphorisms); (2) *geya* (verses in which the same thing is repeated as in the prose part); (3) *vyâkarana* (Buddha's prophecy about Bodhisattva's attainment of Buddhahood in the future); (4) *gâthâ* (independent verses); (5) *udâna* (sermons on Buddha's own account); (6) *nidâna* (sermons as the occasion required); (7) *avadâna* (legends, but according to Chinese interpretation parables); (8) *ityukta* (speeches relating to the former deeds of Bodhisattvas); (9) *jâtaka* (accounts of Buddha's own former lives); (10) *vaipulya* (doctrines of deep significance); (11) *adbhutadharma* (extraordinary phenomena); (12) *upadeça* (expositions).

even if they read only a few of them.   There were
others who by their own intellectual powers could
understand the meanings of the Sûtras only after an
extensive reading of many of them.   Still others lacking in intellectual powers of their own could understand the meanings of the Sûtras only through the assistance of elaborate commentaries.   But there are
some who, lacking in intellectual powers of their own,
shun the perusal of elaborate commentaries and take
delight in studying and cultivating enquiries which
present the many-sidedness and universality of the
doctrine in a concise form.

For the sake of the people of the last class I write
this Discourse, in which the most excellent, the deepest, and the most inexhaustible Doctrine of the Tathâgata will be treated in comprehensive brevity.

II. GENERAL STATEMENT.

In what does the general statement consist?

The Mahâyâna can be briefly treated as to two
aspects, namely, What it is, and What it signifies.[1]

[1] " What is " and " What signifies " are respectively in Chinese *yu fa* 有法 and *fa* 法, but in the older translation *fa* 法
and *i* 義 . This is a little puzzling, but if we bear in mind that in
Chinese as well as in Sanskrit *fa* or *dharma* means both the substance itself and its attribute or significance, or law that regulates
its movements, we will understand that Paramârtha, the first translator, used *fa* here in the sense of substance or " what is," while
Çikshânanda, the second translator, used the word in the sense of
significance or that by which a thing is conceived, the ordinary
meaning of *i*.

What is the Mahâyâna? It is the soul[1] of all sentient beings (*sarvasattva*), that constitutes all things in the world, phenomenal and supra-phenomenal;[2] and through this soul we can disclose what the Mahâyâna signifies.

Because the soul in itself, involving the quintessence of the Mahâyâna, is suchness (*bhûtatathatâ*), but it becomes [in its relative or transitory aspect, through the law of causation] birth-and-death (*samsâra*) in which are revealed the quintessence, the attributes, and the activity of the Mahâyâna.

The Mahâyâna has a triple significance.[3]

The first is the greatness of quintessence. Because the quintessence of the Mahâyâna as suchness

---

[1] "Soul" is not used here in a dualistic sense, but as Dr. Paul Carus defines it in the last chapter of *The Soul of Man*. Speaking of the soul of the universe he defines the term as "the formative principle which gave and still gives shape to the world" (*loc. cit.*, first edition, p. 437). The literal translation of the Chinese character 心 *hsin* is kernel, or heart, or essence of all things. The Chinese *hsin*, however, is rather indiscriminately used in our text for both Sanskrit terms, *Hrdaya* (kernel or heart) and *Citta* (mind, the thinking faculty). These terms are more or less synonymous, especially from Açvaghosha's standpoint, that does not allow the transcendental existence of a metaphysical soul-entity. In this translation soul denotes the absolute aspect of suchness, and mind its relative aspect, wherever this distinction is noticeable.

[2] This is a literal translation of the Chinese *chu shi chien* 出世間. It signifies anything transcending conditionality or worldliness.

[3] This triad which has a striking similarity to Spinoza's conception of substance, attributes and modes, also reminds us of the first principles (*padârtha*) of the Vaiçeshika philosophy, that is, substance (*dravya*), qualities (*guna*), and action (*karma*).

exists in all things, remains unchanged in the pure as
well as in the defiled, is always one and the same
(*samatâ*), neither increases nor decreases, and is void
of distinction.

The second is the greatness of attributes. Here we
have the Tathâgata's[1] womb[2] (*tathâgatagarbha*) which
in exuberance contains immeasurable and innumerable merits (*punya*) as its characteristics.

The third is the greatness of activity, for it [i. e.,
Mahâyâna] produces all kinds of good work in the
world, phenomenal and supra-phenomenal. [Hence
the name *Mahâ*yâna (great vehicle).]

[Again this Dharma is called the Mahâ*yâna* ;] because it is the vehicle[3] (*yâna*) in which all Buddhas

---

[1] Tathâgata literally means one who thus or truly comes. That
the omnipresent principle of suchness could come or go appeared
contradictory and seemed to render an explanation necessary. The
Vajracchedikâ-Sûtra, Max Müller's English translation, Chap.
XXIX : "And again, O Subhûti, if anybody were to say that the
Tathâgata goes, or comes, or stands, or sits, or lies down, he, O
Subhûti, does not understand the meaning of my preaching. And
why ? Because the word Tathâgata means one who does not go
anywhere, and does not come from anywhere ; and therefore he is
called the Tathâgata (truly come), holy and fully enlightened."

[2] Cf. the *Bhavadgîtâ* (*Sacred Books of the East*, Vol. VIII.,
Chap. XIV., p. 107) : "The great Brahman is a womb for me, in
which I cast the seed. From that, O descendant of Bharata ! is
the birth of all things. Of the bodies, O son of Kuntî ! which are
born from all wombs, the main womb is the great Brahman, and I
am the father, the giver of the seed."

[3] Cf. the *Saddharma-pundarîka*, Chap. II. (*Sacred Books
of the East*, Vol. XXI., p. 40): "By means of one sole vehicle, to
wit, the Buddha-vehicle, Çâriputra, do I teach creatures the law;
there is no second, nor a third."

from the beginning have been riding, and Bodhisatt-vas[1] when riding in it will enter into the state of Bud-dhahood.

III. THE EXPLANATION.

In what does the explanation of the general state-ment consist?

This part consists of three subdivisions :

1. The Revelation of the True Doctrine.
2. The Refutation of False Doctrines.
3. The Practice of the Right Path.

1. The Revelation of the True Doctrine.

In the one soul we may distinguish two aspects. The one is the Soul as suchness (*bhûtatathatâ*), the other is the soul as birth-and-death (*samsâra*).   Each in itself constitutes all things, and both are so closely interrelated that one cannot be separated from the other.

A. The Soul as Suchness.

What is meant by the soul as suchness (*bhûtata-thatâ*), is the oneness of the totality of things (*dhar-madhâtu*),[2] the great all-including whole, the quintes-

---

[1] Literally, one who seeks perfect enlightenment, or one who is full of wisdom and compassion.

[2] S. Beal in his English translation of Açvaghosha's *Buddha-carita* (*Sacred Books of the East*, Vol. XIX., p. 324, footnote) considers *dharmadhâtu* to be " the mystic or ideal world of the Northern Buddhists" and says it means literally the "limit of dharma."   The interpretation is evidently wrong, not only because *dhâtu* according to the *Madhyanta-vibhâga-çâstra* by Vasubandhu

sence of the Doctrine.   For the essential nature of
the soul is uncreate and eternal.

All things, simply on account of our confused subjectivity (*smrti*),[1] appear under the forms of individuation.   If we could overcome our confused subjectivity, the signs of individuation would disappear, and
there would be no trace of a world of [individual and
isolated] objects.[2]

Therefore all things in their fundamental nature
are not namable or explicable.   They cannot be adequately expressed in any form of language.   They are

(two Chinese translations : one by Paramârtha A. D. 557–569, and
the other by Hsüan-tsang A. D. 691) means root, base, cause, or
principle ; but because *Dharmadhâtu, fa kai* 法界 in Chinese,
is not used by the Northern Buddhists in the sense that Beal gives.
It means on the other hand this actual world considered from the
point of its forming the basis of the law ; or, to use modern scientific terminology, it is existence in its organised totality.   Açvaghosha uses the term here in this sense.

[1] The term is usually rendered by recollection or memory, but
Açvaghosha uses it apparently in a different sense.   It must mean
subjectivity, or the perception of particularity, or that mental activity which is not in accordance with the suchness of things ; if
otherwise, the whole drift of the present Discourse becomes totally
unintelligible.   *Smrti* is in some degree obviously synonymous
with *Avidya* (ignorance) which is more general and more prim-
ordial than the former.   Ignorance appears first and when it starts
the world-process, "subjectivity" is evolved, which in its turn
causes particularisation to take place.   Particularisation does not
annihilate suchness, but it overshadows the light of its perfect
spiritual wisdom.

[2] Schopenhauer who says, "no subject without object," seems
to express a similar idea that without subjectivity, "the objective
world," i. e., "the world as *Vorstellung*, as representation of objects" would vanish.

without the range of apperception. [They are universals.] They [things in their fundamental nature] have no signs of distinction. [They are not particulars.] They possess absolute sameness (*samatâ*). [They are universals.] They are subject neither to transformation, nor to destruction. They are nothing but the one soul, for which suchness is another designation. Therefore they cannot be [fully] explained by words or exhausted by reasoning.

While all words and expressions are nothing but representations and not realities, and their existence depends simply on our confused subjectivity, suchness has no attribute [of particularity] to speak of. But the term suchness is all that can be expressed in language, and through this term all other terms may be disposed of.

In the essence of suchness, there is neither anything which has to be excluded, nor anything which has to be added.[2]

[1] If I understand Açvaghosha correctly, he intends to say that to the sentient subject the world consists of a number of isolated objects. The nature of subjectivity is sense-apperception ; and in sense-apperception the particular things are represented in the particularity only, not in their suchness as momentarily materialised universals. We must overcome subjectivity in order to discover suchness ; but when suchness is recognised, it is at once understood to constitute the essence and only true reality of things.

[2] The older translation has : "In the essence of suchness, there is nothing to be excluded, for all things are true ; nor is there anything to be added, for all things are such as they are. Be it known therefore that as thus all things are undemonstrable and

Now the question arises : If that be so, how can all beings conform to and have an insight into [suchness]?

The answer is : As soon as you understand that when the totality of existence is spoken of, or thought of, there is neither that which speaks nor that which is spoken of, there is neither that which thinks nor that which is thought of ; then you conform to suchness ; and when your subjectivity is thus completely obliterated, it is said to have the insight.

Again there is a twofold aspect in suchness if viewed from the point of its explicability. The first is trueness as negation (*çûnyatâ*),[1] in the sense that

unrepresentable [by our confused understanding], they are called suchness."

[1] The term *çûnyatâ* which means literally void or emptiness, has suffered a great deal of misunderstanding by those who are not well acquainted with Buddhist phraseology. If Mahâyânists used the term, as imagined by some critics, in the sense of absolute nothingness, denying the existence of everything conditional as well as unconditional, relative as well as independent, how could they speak about the highest truth (*paramârthasatya*) or the most excellent perfect enlightenment (*anuttarasamyaksambodhi*) which all conveys the sense of affirmation ? What the Çûnyatâ doctrine positively insists on, is the denial of sensationalism, and the annihilation of the imagination that weaves a dualistic world-conception. If this could be called a nihilism, every intellectual attempt to reach a unitary view of the universe would be nihilistic, for it declares the untenability of a separate existence of matter and thought, me and not-me, etc. It is odd enough that such a self-evident truth should have escaped the keen observance of Christian critics. Açvaghosha here states that the bhûtatathatâ is at once çûnya and açûnya. It is çûnya because it transcends all forms of separation and individuation ; it is açûnya because all possible things in the world emanate from it. Even Nâgârjuna

it is completely set apart from the attributes of all
things unreal, that it is the real reality. The second
is trueness as affirmation (*açûnyatâ*), in the sense that
it contains infinite merits, that it is self-existent.

And again by trueness as negation we mean that
in its [metaphysical] origin it has nothing to do with
things defiled [i. e., conditional], that it is free from
all signs of distinction existing among phenomenal
objects, that it is independent of unreal, particularising consciousness.

Thus we understand that suchness (*bhûtatathatâ*)
is neither that which is existence, nor that which is
non-existence, nor that which is at once existence and
non-existence, nor that which is not at once existence
and non-existence; that it is neither that which is
unity, nor that which is plurality, nor that which is at
once unity and plurality, nor that which is not at once
unity and plurality.[1]

who is supposed to be the founder of the nihilistic Prajñâpâramitâ
system by Christian students of Buddhism, says in his *Mâdhyamika-çâstra*, Chap. XXII., that the idea of çûnyatâ and that of
açûnyatâ are both wrong, but that from the deficiency of language
to denote the exact state of things he has made use of these terms.
(Observe that Açvaghosha says the very same thing in the preceding passages.) Nâgârjuna therefore apparently had something in
his mind to define, but that something having nothing in common
with things we daily encounter in our sense-world, he designated
it çûnya, empty, and he hoped by thus abnegating all phenomenal
existences, we could reach the highest reality, for ignorant minds
are deeply saturated with wrong affirmations and false judgements.

[1] Cf. Nâgârjuna's "Eight No's" doctrine which says: "There
is no production (*utpâda*), no destruction (*uccheda*), no annihilation (*nirodha*), no persistence (*çâçvata*), no unity (*ekârtha*), no

In a word, as suchness cannot be comprehended by the particularising consciousness of all beings, we call it the negation [or nothingness, *çûnyatâ*].

The truth is that subjectivity does not exist by itself, that the negation (*çûnyatâ*) is also void (*çûnya*) in its nature, that neither that which is negated [viz., the external world] nor that which negates [viz., the mind] is an independent entity.[1]

By the so-called trueness as affirmation, we mean that [as soon as we understand] subjectivity is empty and unreal, we perceive the pure soul manifesting itself as eternal, permanent, immutable and completely comprising all things that are pure. On that account we call it affirmation [or reality, or non-emptiness, *açûnyatâ*]. Nevertheless, there is no trace of affirmation in it, because it is not the product of a confused subjectivity, because only by transcending subjectivity (*smrti*) can it be grasped.

b. *The Soul as Birth-and-Death.*

The soul as birth-and-death (*samsâra*) comes forth [as the law of causation] from the Tathâgata's womb (*Tathâgatagarbha*). But the immortal [i. e., such-

plurality (*nânârtha*), no coming in (*âgamana*), no going out (*nirgama*)." The statement means that pure truth (*paramârtha*) transcends all modes of relativity. (See the first chapter of the *Mâdhyamika-çâstra*.)

[1] In the Kantian sense of "things in themselves." The Mâdhyamika school would say they are all *Atyanta-çûnyatâ*, complete void, meaning that things are subject to transformation and have no absolute existence.

ness] and the mortal [i. e., birth-and-death] coincide
with each other.[1] Though they are not identical, they
are not a duality. [Thus when the absolute soul assumes a relative aspect by its self-affirmation] it is
called the all-conserving mind (*âlaya-vijñâna*).[2]

The same mind has a twofold significance as the
organiser and the producer of all things.

Again it embraces two principles: (1) Enlightenment; (2) Non-enlightenment.

Enlightenment is the highest quality of the mind;
it is free from all [the limiting] attributes of subjectivity (*smrti*). As it is free from all [limiting] attri-

---

[1] Cf. the *Bhagavadgîtâ*, Chap. IX., p. 84: "I am immortality
and also death; and I, O Arjuna! am that which is and that which
is not." See also Chap. X., p. 90.

[2] *Âlaya* or *Alaya* comes from the root *lî*, which means: ad-
here; melt, dissolve; sit upon, dwell in, stay in, etc.; while its
nominal form *laya* means: act of clinging; melting, fusion, solution, dissolution; rest, repose; place of rest, residence, house,
dwelling. According to Paramârtha, who belongs to the so-called
"Older Translators," the original Sanskrit equivalent of the "all-
conserving mind" seems to be *alaya* or *aliya*, for he translates it
by *Wu mo shih*, not-disappearing mind, in the sense that this
mind retains everything in it. But Hsüan-tsang, the leader of the
"New Translators," renders it by *tsang shih*, that is, the mind
that hoards or preserves, or dwelling-mind or receptacle-mind,
according to which the original seems to be *âlaya*, or *laya* with
the prefix *â* instead of its negative form with the particle *a*. The
ultimate significance of the term in question, however, does not
materially differ, whether it is *wu mo*, not-disappearing, or *tsang*,
house, place of keeping things. My translation of the same is
rather liberal, in order to make it more intelligible to the general
reader. Some other names given to the *âlaya-vijnâna* are *citta*,
mind; *âdâna*, the supporting; *âçraya*, foundation or seeds.

butes of subjectivity, it is like unto space (*âkâça*), penetrating everywhere, as the unity of all (*dharma-dhâtu*). That is to say, it is the universal Dharma-kâya[1] of all Tathâgatas.

On account of this Dharmakâya, all Tathâgatas are spoken of as abiding in enlightenment *a priori*.

Enlightenment *a priori* is contrasted with enlightenment *a posteriori*. Through enlightenment *a posteriori* is gained no more than enlightenment *a priori*.

Now we speak of enlightenment *a posteriori*; because there is enlightenment *a priori*, there is non-

---

[1] There seems to be a general misconception about the exact significance of the term *Dharmakâya* which constitutes the central point of the Mahâyâna system. Most Western Buddhist scholars render it the Body or Personality of the Law, understanding by law the doctrine of Buddha. This may be correct in the Southern Buddhism as well as in its historical sense, because after the Nirvâna of Buddha it was quite natural for his disciples to personify the doctrine of their teacher, as their now only living spiritual leader. But in the course of time it acquired entirely different significance and ceased to mean the personification of the Doctrine. Now *dharma*, as aforesaid, does not only mean law or doctrine, but also it means an individual object, an idea, a substance, or, when it is used in its broadest sense, existence in general. *Kâya* means a body or person, but not in the sense of an animated, sentient being; it denotes a system in which parts are connected, a unified whole, that which forms a basis, etc. Dharma-kâya therefore signifies that which constitutes the ultimate foundation of existence, one great whole in which all forms of individuation are obliterated, in a word, the Absolute. This objective absolute being meanwhile has been idealised by Mahâyânists so that that which knows is now identical with that which is known, because they say that the essence of existence is nothing but intelligence pure, perfect, and free from all possible worries and evils.

enlightenment, and because there is non-enlightenment we can speak of enlightenment *a posteriori.*

Again, when the mind is enlightened as to its own
ultimate nature, it is called perfect enlightenment;
when it is not enlightened as to its ultimate nature, it
is not perfect enlightenment.

Common people[1] (*prthagjana*), who, becoming
conscious of errors that occur in a succession of their
mental states, abstain from making conclusions, may
be spoken of as enlightened; but in reality theirs is
non-enlightenment.

Çrâvakas,[2] Pratyekabuddhas, and those Bodhi-

[1] *Prthagjana* has a technical sense in Buddhism, for any one
that is ignorant of the doctrine of non-âtman and commits all
those actions which lead one to a constant transmigration, is
counted among the *profanum vulgus*, to distinguish him from the
Çrâvaka, Pratyekabuddha, and Bodhisattva.

[2] The *Saddharmapundarîka-Sûtra* contains an explanation
of these terms generally adopted by Mahâyânists, which read as
follows (see Kern's English translation of the same, Chap. III., p.
80): "Now, Çâriputra, the beings who have become wise have
faith in the Tathâgata, the father of the world, and consequently
apply themselves to his commandments. Amongst them there are
some who, wishing to follow the dictates of an authoritative voice,
apply themselves to the commandment of the Tathâgata to acquire
the knowledge of the *four great truths*, for the sake of *their own*
complete Nirvâna. These one may say to be those who, coveting
the vehicle of the disciple (Çrâvaka), fly from the triple world." . . .
This is the definition given to the Çrâvakayâna. We proceed next
to that of the Pratyekabuddhayâna: "Other beings, desirous of
the science without a master, of self-restraint and tranquillity, apply themselves to the commandment of the Tathâgata to learn to
understand *causes and effects* (*i. e., the twelve chains of relation*) for the sake of *their own* complete Nirvâna. These one may
say to be those who, coveting the vehicle of the Pratyekabuddha,

sattvas who have just entered their course, recognising the difference between subjectivity and the trans-
scending of subjectivity both in essence and attributes, have become emancipated from the coarse form
of particularisation.   This is called enlightenment in
appearance.

Bodhisattvas of the Dharmakâya,[1] having recognised that subjectivity and the transcending of subjectivity have no reality of their own [i. e., are rela-
tive], have become emancipated from the intermediate
form of particularisation.   This is called approximate
enlightenment.

Those who have transcended the stage of Bodhisattvahood and attained the ultimate goal, possess a
consciousness which is consistent and harmonious ;

fly from the triple world." . . . Those who belong to these two
classes desire to achieve only the salvation of their own, and not
that of all mankind, in which respect Bodhisattvas stand far superior to them.   We read in the same Sûtra to the following effect :
"Others again, desirous of the knowledge of the all-knowing, the
knowledge of Buddha, the knowledge of the self-born one, the science without a master, apply themselves to the commandment of
the Tathâgata to learn to understand the knowledge, powers, and
freedom from hesitation, of the Tathâgata, for the sake of the
*common weal and happiness, out of compassion to the world,
for the benefit, weal, and happiness of the world at large, both
gods and men, for the sake of the complete Nirvâna of all beings.*   These one may say to be those who, coveting the great
vehicle (mahâyâna), fly from the triple world.   Therefore they are
called Bodhisattva Mahâsattva."   (The italics are mine.)

[1] Those who have recognised the all-prevailing Dharmakâya,
but who have not as yet been able to perfectly identify themselves
with it.

they have recognised the origin from which consciousness [or mentation] starts.[1]   This will truly be called
enlightenment.

Having transcended the attributes of enlightenment and the subtlest form of particularisation, they
[i. e., Buddhas] have gained a perfect and eternal insight into the very nature of the soul [i. e., suchness],
because the latter now presents itself to them in its
absolute and immutable form.[2]   Therefore they are
called Tathâgatas, and theirs is perfect enlightenment ; and therefore it is said in the Sûtra[3] that those
who have an insight into the non-reality of all subjectivity, attain to the wisdom of the Tathâgata.

In the preceding statement we referred to the origin
from which consciousness [or mentation] starts according to the popular expression.   In truth there is
no such thing as the origin of consciousness [or men-
tation]; for consciousness [being purely subjective]
has no absolute [but only a phenomenal] existence.
How can we then speak of its origin?

The multitude of people (*bahujana*) are said to be

[1] Consciousness, i. e., mentation or mental activity, is transient, it takes place in time, and must not be confused with soul,
or suchness, or eternal wisdom.

[2] In the older translation these passages are somewhat sim-
plified.

[3] The *Lankâvatâra Sûtra*.   There are three Chinese translations of the same still extant among the Japanese Tripitaka collection : (1) by Guṇabhadra, A. D. 443, four fasciculi ; (2) by Bo-
dhiruci, A. D. 513, ten fasciculi ; (3) by Çikshânanda, A. D. 700-
704, seven fasciculi

lacking in enlightenment, because ignorance (*avidya*) prevails there from all eternity, because there is a constant succession of confused subjective states (*smrti*) from which they have never been emancipated.

But when they transcend their subjectivity, they can then recognise that all states of mentation, viz., their appearance, presence, change, and disappearance [in the field of consciousness] have no [genuine] reality.[1]   They are neither in a temporal nor in a spatial relation with the one soul,[2] for they are not self-existent.

When you understand this, you also understand that enlightenment *a posteriori* cannot be manufactured, for it is no other thing than enlightenment *a priori* [which is uncreate and must be discovered].[3]

And again enlightenment *a priori*, when implicated in the domain of defilement [i. e., relativity], is differentiated into two kinds of attributes :

(1) Pure wisdom (*prajñâ?*) ; (2) Incomprehensible activity (*karma?*).[4]

---

[1] The older translation differs a little, but agrees in the main.

[2] The older translation reads : " The four states of mentation are simultaneous [they belong together in time, i. e., they are in uninterrupted succession], but have no self-existence, because enlightenment *a priori* always remains in its sameness."

[3] This passage is wanting in the older translation.

[4] The differentiation of enlightenment into two distinct qualities, wisdom and action, or, according to the terminology of later Mahâyânists, wisdom and love, constitutes one of the principal thoughts of the Mahâyâna Buddhism and shows a striking similarity to the Christian conception of God who is considered to be full of infinite love and wisdom.

By pure wisdom we understand that when one, by virtue of the perfuming[1] power of the Dharma, disciplines himself truthfully [i. e., according to the Dharma], and accomplishes meritorious deeds, the mind [i. e., *âlaya-vijñâna*] which implicates itself with birth-and-death will be broken down, and the modes of the evolving-consciousness[2] will be annulled; while the pure and genuine wisdom of the Dharmakâya manifests itself.[3]

Though all modes of consciousness and mentation are mere products of ignorance, ignorance in its ultimate nature is identical and not-identical[4] with enlightenment *a priori;* and therefore ignorance in one sense is destructible, while in the other sense it is indestructible.

This may be illustrated by [the simile of] the water and the waves which are stirred up in the ocean. Here the water can be said to be identical [in one sense] and not-identical [in the other sense][5] with the waves. The waves are stirred up by the wind, but the water remains the same. When the wind ceases, the motion of the waves subsides; but the water remains the same.

[1] This term will be explained later on. See p. 84.

[2] For the explanation see below, p. 76.

[3] Note that the Dharmakâya is not the "Body of the Law," but suchness (*bhûtatathatâ*) itself, which transcends the limits of time and space as well as the law of causation.

[4] Literally, "neither identical nor not-identical."

[5] Literally, "neither identical nor not-identical."

Likewise, when the mind of all creatures which in its own nature is pure and clean, is stirred up by the wind of ignorance (*avidya*), the waves of mentality (*vijñâna*) make their appearance. These three [i. e., the mind, ignorance, and mentality], however, have no [absolute] existence, and they are neither unity nor plurality.[1]

But the mind though pure in its essence is the source of the awakened [or disturbed] mentality. When ignorance is annihilated, the awakened mentality is tranquilised, whilst the essence of the wisdom remains unmolested.[2]

Incomprehensible activity which we know proceeds from pure wisdom, uninterruptedly produces all excellent spiritual states. That is to say, the personality (*kâya*) of the Tathâgata,[3] which in exuberance contains immeasurable and ever-growing merits, reveals itself to all beings according to their various predispositions [or characters], and accomplishes for them innumerable [spiritual] benefits.

Further there is a fourfold significance in the na-

[1] That is, they are one in one sense, but different in the other sense.

[2] In the older translation the last two paragraphs read :

"Likewise the mind of all beings though clean and pure in its own nature is disturbed [or awakened] through the wind of ignorance. Neither the mind nor ignorance has any form and attribute [of its own]. They condition each other. But the mind itself not being the principle of disturbance its movability will cease when ignorance is gone, though its essence, wisdom, remains unmolested."

[3] Or the *Tathâgatagarbha*.

ture of enlightenment whose purity may be likened unto space or a bright mirror.

The first great significance which may be likened unto space and a bright mirror, is trueness as negation (*çûnyatâ*), in the sense that enlightenment is absolutely unobtainable by any modes of relativity or by any outward signs of enlightenment.

The second great significance which may be likened unto space and a bright mirror, is trueness as affirmation (*açûnyatâ*), in the sense that all things [in their ultimate nature] are perfect and complete, and not subject to destruction ; in the sense that all events in the phenomenal world are reflected in enlightenment, so that they neither pass out of it, nor enter into it, and that they neither disappear nor are destroyed ; that they are in one eternal and immutable soul which by none of the defiled things can be defiled and whose wisdom-essence enveloping immeasurable and innumerable merits, becomes the cause of perfuming the minds of all beings.

The third great significance which may be likened unto space and a bright mirror, is the affirmation as free from the hindrances (*âvarana*), in the sense that enlightenment is forever cut off from the hindrances both affectional (*kleçâvarana*) and intellectual (*jñeyâvarana*), as well as from the mind [i. e., *âlaya-vijñâna*] which implicates itself with birth-and-death, since it is in its true nature clean, pure, eternal, calm, and immutable.

The fourth great significance which may be likened unto space and a bright mirror, is the affirmation as unfolding itself, in the sense that on account of a liberation from the hindrances, it transforms and unfolds itself, wherever conditions are favorable, in the form of a Tathâgata or in some other forms, in order that all beings might be induced thereby to bring their root[1] of merit (*kuçalamûla*) to maturity.[2]

By the so-called non-enlightenment, we mean that as the true Dharma [i. e., suchness] is from all eternity not truthfully recognised in its oneness, there issues forth an unenlightened mind and then subjectivity (*smrti*). But this subjectivity has no self-existence independent of enlightenment *a priori*.

To illustrate : a man who is lost goes astray because he is bent on pursuing a certain direction ; and his confusion has no valid foundation other than that he is bent on a certain direction.

It is even the same with all beings. They become

[1] Max Müller renders the term by "stock of merit," but I think "stock" is not very fitly adopted to denote the sense usually attached to it by Buddhists. According to them, karma, be it meritorious or not-meritorious, has an efficient power to bear the fruit; therefore every act done by us like the root of a plant has a regenerative force potentially reserved within itself, and does not, like a stock of things which are not necessarily alive, remain dormant lacking productive powers in it.

[2] According to the older translation, the first significance is called the "mirror of transcendental (or empty) trueness"; the second, the "mirror of the perfuming principle"; the third, the "mirror of the dharma of liberation"; and the fourth, the "mirror of the perfuming cause."

unenlightened, foster their subjectivity and go astray, because they are bent on enlightenment. But non-enlightenment has no existence of its own, aside from its relation with enlightenment *a priori*. And as enlightenment *a priori* is spoken of only in contrast to non-enlightenment, and as non-enlightenment is a non-entity, true enlightenment in turn loses its significance too. [That is to say, they are simply relative.]

In blindness[1] there arose non-enlightenment of which three aspects are to be noted. These three are not independent.

The first aspect is ignorant action (*avidyakarma?*).[2] A disturbance[3] of the mind [i. e., *âlaya-vijñâna*] caused by non-enlightenment characterises the beginning of karma. When enlightened, the mind is no more dis-

[1] Rather "carelessness." This is missing in the older translation.

[2] The term "ignorant action" reminds us of Schopenhauer's "blind will" and we might translate the Chinese terms *pu chiao* 不覺 ignorant or unconscious, by "blind." On the other hand, the expression reminds one of Goethe's words in Faust: "Im Anfang war die That," i. e., in the beginning there was karma; and this karma starting in an unenlightened condition was blind or ignorant, it was as yet unconscious of its goal which is the attainment of the eternal truth, the discovery of enlightenment *a priori*. Cf. also the *Chândogya Upanisad*, VI, 2.

[3] By "disturbance" is meant that the mind or soul, awaking from a state of perfect sameness and tranquillity, discriminates the subject and the object, me and not-me. The "disturbance" itself, however, is neither good nor bad; the fault lies in clinging to this dual aspect of existence as absolute, utterly ignoring their fundamental identity. Efface the clinging from your mind, and you are purified and saved.

turbed. But by its disturbance misery (*duhkha*) is produced according to the law of causation.

The second aspect is that which perceives [i. e., the ego or subject]. In consequence of the disturbance of the mind there originates that which perceives an external world. When the mind is not disturbed, perception does not take place.

The third aspect is the external world. Through perception an unreal external world originates. Independent of that which perceives [i. e., the ego or subject], there is no surrounding world [or the object].[1]

Conditioned by the unreal external world, six kinds of phenomena arise in succession.

The first phenomenon is intelligence [i. e., sensation]. Being affected by the external world the mind becomes conscious of the difference between the agreeable and the disagreeable.

The second phenomenon is succession [i. e., memory]. Following upon intelligence, memory retains the sensations agreeable as well as disagreeable in a continuous succession of subjective states.

The third phenomenon is clinging. Through the retention and succession of sensations agreeable as well as disagreeable, there arises the desire of clinging.

The fourth phenomenon is an attachment to names

---

[1] This is the idealistic phase of the Mahâyâna Buddhism. Berkeley says: "Take away the perceiving mind and you take away the objective world."

[or ideas, *samjñâ*], etc.[1]   By clinging the mind hypostasises all names whereby to give definitions to all
things.

The fifth phenomenon is the performance of deeds
(*karma*).   On account of attachment to names, etc.,
there arise all the variations of deeds, productive of
individuality.

The sixth phenomenon is the suffering due to the
fetter of deeds.   Through deeds suffering arises in
which the mind finds itself entangled and curtailed of
its freedom.

Be it therefore known that all defiled things do
not exist by themselves, for all of them have arisen
from ignorance.

Now there is a twofold relation between enlightenment and non-enlightenment: (1) identity; (2) non-
identity.

The relation of identity may be illustrated by the

---

[1] Here is again a strange agreement with Western philosophy.
The nominalists speak of names as mere *flatus vocis* and the things-
in-themselves (i. e., what is conceived by names) are declared to
be unknowable by Kant.   Dr. Paul Carus goes one step further by
declaring that there are no things-in-themselves, but forms-in-
themselves, viz., the eternal types of beings or Plato's ideas.   The
clinging to names is based on the metaphysical error of interpret-
ing names as entities or things-in-themselves, which exhibits the
nominalistic phase of Buddhism.   On the other hand, the strong
emphasis laid on the reality of suchness, or what Dr. Carus calls
the purely formal, shows the realistic phase of Buddhism.   The
word "hypostasises" used in the next passage means literally in
the younger translation "firmly builds a basis for," in the older
one we read literally "one sets separately forth what is unreal,
i. e., names and words."

simile of all kinds of pottery which though different are all made of the same clay. Likewise the undefiled (*anâçrava*)[1] and ignorance (*avidya*) and their various transcient forms come all from one and the same entity. Therefore Buddha teaches[2] that all beings are from all eternity ever abiding in Nirvâna.[3] In truth enlightenment cannot be manufactured, nor can it be created; it is absolutely intangible; it is no material existence that is an object of sensation.

The reason why enlightenment nevertheless assumes tangible material form is that it suffers defilement[4] which is the source of all transient forms of manifestation. Wisdom itself has nothing to do with material phenomena whose characteristic feature is

[1] A dharma not subject to the transformation of birth and death is called 無漏 *wu lou* in Chinese and *anâçrava* in Sanskrit. It is commonly used in contrast to 有漏 *yu lou* and *sâçrava*, which means " defiled " or " conditional."

[2] This teaching is set forth in the fourth chapter of the *Vimalakîrtinirdeça Sûtra*, one of the most popular Mahâyâna texts in China as well as in Japan. There are several Chinese translations still extant, the earliest of which was produced during the first half of the third century of the Christian era.

[3] Observe that Nirvâna is here used as a synonym of suchness (*bhûtatathatâ*).

[4] That is to say, being mixed up in the material world. "Defilement " does not necessarily mean evil or immorality. Anything that does not come directly from the fountain-head of suchness, but is in some way or other "perfumed " by ignorance, the principle of individuation, is called defiled or impure. From the ethical point of view it may be good or bad, according to our subjective attitude towards it. All that should be avoided is a clinging to the phenomenal existence.

extension in space, and there are no attributes there by which wisdom can become tangible. This is the meaning of Buddha's brief statement just referred to.

The relation of non-identity may be illustrated by the difference that obtains among the various kinds of pottery. The relation among the undefiled and ignorance and their various transient forms of manifestation is similar to it.

And again, by the law of causation (*hetupratyaya*) in the domain of birth-and-death (*samsâra*) we mean that depending on the mind [i. e., *âlaya-vijñâna*] an evolution of the ego (*manas*) and consciousness (*vijñâna*)[1] takes place in all beings.

What is meant by this?

In the all-conserving mind (*âlaya-vijñâna*) ignorance obtains; and from the non-enlightenment starts that which sees, that which represents, that which apprehends an objective world, and that which constantly particularises. This is called the ego (*manas*).

---

[1] *Manovijñâna* in the older translation. Now *vijñâna* (or *manovijñâna*), *manas* and *citta* are to a certain extent synonymous and interchangeable, as all designating that which feels, thinks and wills, or what is commonly called mind. According to a general interpretation of Mahâyânists, the following distinction is made among them: *citta*, mind, is more fundamental, somehow corresponding to the conception of the soul, for it has the inherent capacity for ideation as well as for the power of storing up within itself the results of experience; the most characteristic feature of the *manas*, the ego, is to constantly reflect on itself and to unconsciously assert the existence of the ego; the *vijñâna*, consciousness, is principally the faculty of feeling, perceiving, discriminating, judging, etc., in short, general mental activity or consciousness.

Five different names are given to the ego [according to its different modes of operation].

The first name is activity-consciousness (*Karma-vijñâna?*) in the sense that through the agency of ignorance an unenlightened mind begins to be disturbed [or awakened].

The second name is evolving-consciousness [*pra-vrtti-vijñâna*, i. e., the subject], in the sense that when the mind is disturbed, there evolves that which sees an external world.

The third name is representation-consciousness, in the sense that the ego (*manas*) represents [or reflects] an external world. As a clean mirror reflects the images of all description, it is even so with the representation-consciousness. When it is confronted, for instance, with the five objects of sense, it represents them at once, instantaneously, and without any effort.

The fourth name is particularisation-consciousness, in the sense that it discriminates between different things defiled as well as pure.

The fifth name is succession-consciousness [i. e., memory], in the sense that continuously directed by the awakening consciousness [or attention, *manaskara*] it [*manas*] retains and never loses or suffers the destruction of any karma, good as well as evil, which had been sown in the past, and whose retribution, painful as well as agreeable, it never fails to mature, be it in the present or in the future; and also in the

sense that it unconsciously recollects things gone by,
and in imagination anticipates things to come.

Therefore the three domains[1] (*triloka*) are nothing
but the self-manifestation of the mind [i. e., *âlaya-
vijñâna* which is practically identical with suchness,
bhûtatathatâ].[2] Separated from the mind, there would
be no such things as the six objects of sense.

Why?

Since all things, owing the principle of their existence to the mind (*âlaya-vijñâna*), are produced by
subjectivity (*smrti*), all the modes of particularisation
are the self-particularisation of the mind. The mind
in itself [or the soul] being, however, free from all
attributes, is not differentiated. Therefore we come
to the conclusion that all things and conditions in the
phenomenal world, hypostasised and established only
through ignorance (*avidya*) and subjectivity (*smrti*)
on the part of all beings, have no more reality than
the images in a mirror.[3] They evolve simply from

---

[1] They are: (1) Domain of feeling (*kâmaloka*); (2) Domain of
bodily existence (*rûpaloka*); (3) Domain of incorporeality (*arûpaloka*).

[2] The mind or *âlaya-vijñâna* is suchness (or, as Dr. Carus
would say, "purely formal thought,") in its operation, where it
may be called the rational principle in nature or the *Gesetzmässigkeit* of the cosmos. It manifests itself not only in human reason, but appears also as the principle of individuation, determin-
ing all particular forms of existence, as will be explained in the
following lines.

[3] Compare Schopenhauer's conception of the world as *Vorstellung*.

the ideality of a particularising mind. When the mind
is disturbed, the multiplicity of things is produced;
but when the mind is quieted, the multiplicity of
things disappears.

By ego-consciousness (*manovijñâna*) we mean that
all ignorant minds through their succession-consciousness cling to the conception of *I* and *not-I* [i. e., a
separate objective world] and misapprehend the nature of the six objects of sense. The ego-consciousness is also called separation-consciousness, or phenomena-particularising-consciousness, because it is
nourished by the perfuming[1] influence of the prejudices (*âçrava*), intellectual as well as affectional.

The mind [or consciousness, *vijñâna*] that starts
from the perfuming influence of ignorance which has
no beginning cannot be comprehended by the intellect of common people (*prthagjana*), Çrâvakas and
Pratyekabuddhas.

It is partially comprehended by those Bodhisattvas
at the stage of knowledge-and-practice, who discipline
themselves, practise contemplation and become the
Bodhisattvas of the Dharmakâya; while even those
who have reached the highest stage of Bodhisattvahood cannot thoroughly comprehend it.

The only one who can have a clear and consummate knowledge of it is the Tathâgata.[2]

[1] The term will be explained later.

[2] The same idea is expressed in the *Crîmâlâ Sûtra* as well as
in the *Lankâvatara Sûtra* where Buddha preaches the unfathom-

Why?

While the essence of the mind is eternally clean
and pure, the influence of ignorance makes possible
the existence of a defiled mind. But in spite of the
defiled mind, the mind [itself] is eternal, clear, pure,
and not subject to transformation.

Further as its original nature is free from particularisation, it knows in itself no change whatever,
though it produces everywhere the various modes of
existence.

When the oneness of the totality of things (*dharmadhâtu*) is not recognised, then ignorance as well as
particularisation arises, and all phases of the defiled
mind are thus developed. But the significance of this
doctrine is so extremely deep and unfathomable that

---

ableness of the nature of suchness which, though pure in its essence, is yet subject to defilement or conditionality,—the mystery
that can be comprehended only by a fully enlightened mind. Referring to this incomprehensibility of the relation of suchness and
ignorance, let me quote what Herbert Spencer says in his *First
Principles* (American ed., p. 45): "For every religion, setting out
though it does with tacit assertion of a mystery, forthwith proceeds
to give some solution of this mystery ; and so asserts that it is not
a mystery passing human comprehension. But an examination of
the solutions they severally propose, shows them to be uniformly
invalid. The analysis of every possible hypothesis proves, not
simply that no hypothesis is sufficient, but that no hypothesis is
even thinkable. And thus the mystery which all religions recognise, turns out to be a far more transcendent mystery than any of
them suppose—not a relative, but an absolute mystery." Is not
the relation of suchness and ignorance the very mystery to which
Spencer makes the allusion here ? Açvaghosha's solution is that
only Buddha can grasp it.

it can be fully comprehended by Buddhas and by no others. Now there are six different phases of the defiled[1] mind thus developed :

1. Interrelated [or secondary] defilement by attachment, from which Çrâvakas, Pratyekabuddhas and those Bodhisattvas at the stage of faith-adaptation can be freed.

2. Interrelated [or secondary] defilement by succession, from which Bodhisattvas with strenuous efforts at the stage of faith, can partially be freed, and at the stage of pure-heartedness, completely.

3. Interrelated [or secondary] defilement by the particularising intelligence, from which Bodhisattvas are gradually freed during their advancement from the stage of morality to the stage of wisdom, while upon reaching the stage of spirituality, they are eternally freed from it.

4. Non-interrelated [or primary] defilement by be-

---

[1] The defilement which is the product of the evolution of the *âlaya-vijnâna*, is of two kinds, primary and secondary. The primary defilement is *a priori*, originating with the birth of the mind. There is as yet no distinct consciousness in it of the duality of the subject and the object, though this is of course tacitly asserted. Açvaghosha calls the primary defilement "non-interrelated," meaning that there is no deliberate reflexion in the ego to assert itself. The secondary defilement called "interrelated" on the other hand explicitly assumes the ego in contradistinction to the non-ego and firmly clings to this conception, which brings forth all selfish desires and actions on the part of the defiled mind. The former being more fundamental than the latter is completely effaced from the mind only after going through all different stages of religious discipline.

lief in an external world, which can be exterminated
at the stage of matter-emancipation.

5. Non-interrelated [or primary] defilement by belief in a perceiving mind, which can be exterminated
at the stage of mind-emancipation.

6. Non-interrelated [or primary] defilement by the
fundamental activity, which can be exterminated in
entering upon the stage of Tathâgatahood, passing
through the highest stage of Bodhisattvahood.

From not recognising the oneness of the totality
of things (*dharmadhâtu*), Bodhisattvas can partially
be liberated by passing first from the stage of faith
and the stage of contemplation to the stage of pure-
heartedness ; while when they enter upon the stage
of Tathâgatahood, they can once for all put an end
[to the illusion].

By "interrelated" we mean that there is [in this
case] a distinction [or consciousness of a duality] between the mind in itself and particularisation, that
there is [here] a distinction [or consciousness of a
duality] between the defiled and the pure, [and there-
fore] that there is [here] an interrelation between that
which perceives and that which determines.

By "non-interrelated" we mean that the mind [in
this case] is perfectly identified with non-enlightenment, so that there is no distinction [or consciousness
of a duality] between these two, [and therefore] that
there is no consciousness of interrelation between that
which perceives and that which determines.

The defiled mind is called affectional hindrance (*kleçâvarana*), because it obscures the fundamental wisdom of suchness (*bhûtatathatâ*). Ignorance is called intellectual hindrance (*jñeyâvarana*), because it obscures the spontaneous exercise of wisdom from which evolve all modes of activity in the world.

What is meant by this?

On account of the defiled mind attachment affirms itself in innumerable ways; and there arises a distinction [or consciousness] between that which apprehends and that which is apprehended. Thus believing in the external world produced by subjectivity, the mind becomes oblivious of the principle of sameness (*samatâ*) that underlies all things.

The essence of all things is one and the same, perfectly calm and tranquil, and shows no sign of becoming; ignorance, however, is in its blindness and delusion oblivious of enlightenment, and, on that account, cannot recognise truthfully all those conditions, differences, and activities which characterise the phenomena of the universe.

Further we distinguish two phases of the self-manifestation of the mind [i. e., *âlaya-vijñâna*, under the law of causation] as birth-and-death (*samsâra*). The first is the cruder phase, being the state of an interrelated mind; the second is the more refined phase, being the state of a non-interrelated mind. The crudest phase is the subjective condition of common people (*prthagjana*); the more refined of the crude or the cruder of the refined is the subjective state of a Bodhisattva.[1] These two phases [of the *âlaya-vijñâna* as the principle of birth-and-death] originate through the perfuming power of ignorance.

The birth-and-death (*samsâra*) has its *raison d'être* (*hetu*) and its cause [or condition, *pratyaya*]. Non-enlightenment is the *raison d'être*, and the external world as produced by subjectivity is the condition. When the *raison d'être* is annihilated, the condition is annihilated [i. e., loses its conditioning power]. When the condition is annihilated, the state of an interrelated mind is annihilated. When the *raison d'être* is annihilated, the state of a non-interrelated mind [too] is annihilated.

It may be asked: If the mind be annihilated, how can there be mentation? If mentation really occurs, how can there be annihilation?

In reply we say that while the objection is well founded, we understand by the annihilation, not that of the mind itself, but of its modes [only].

To illustrate: the water shows the symptoms of disturbance when stirred up by the wind. Have the wind annihilated, and the symptoms of disturbance on the water will also be annihilated, the water itself remaining the same. Let the water itself, however, be annihilated, the symptoms of disturbance would no more be perceptible; because there is nothing

[1] The older translation adds: The most refined of the refined is the spiritual state of a Buddha.

there through which it can show itself. Only so long as the water is not annihilated, the symptoms of disturbance may continue.

It is even the same with all beings. Through ignorance their minds become disturbed. Let ignorance be annihilated, and the symptom of disturbance will also be annihilated, while the essence of the mind [i. e., suchness] remains the same. Only if the mind itself were annihilated, then all beings would cease to exist, because there would be nothing there by which they could manifest themselves. But so long as the mind be not annihilated, its disturbance may continue.

A constant production of things defiled and pure is taking place on account of the inter-perfuming of the four different powers which are as follows: the first is the pure dharma, that is, suchness (*bhûtatathatâ*); the second is the principle of defilement, that is, ignorance (*avidya*); the third is the subjective mind, that is, activity-consciousness (*karmavijñâna?*); the fourth is the external world (*vishaya*) of subjectivity, that is, the six objects of sense.

By "perfuming" we mean that while our worldly clothes [viz., those which we wear] have no odor of their own, neither offensive nor agreeable, they acquire one or the other according to the nature of the substance with which they are perfumed.

Now suchness is a pure dharma free from defilement. It acquires, however, a quality of defilement owing to the perfuming power of ignorance. On the other hand, ignorance has nothing to do with purity. Nevertheless, we speak of its being able to do the work of purity, because it in its turn is perfumed by suchness.

How are defiled things continually produced by perfuming?

Determined by suchness [in its relative aspect], ignorance becomes the *raison d'être* of all forms of defilement. And this ignorance perfumes suchness, and, by perfuming suchness, it produces subjectivity (*smrti*). This subjectivity in its turn perfumes ignorance. On account of this [reciprocal] perfuming, the truth is misunderstood. On account of its being misunderstood, an external world of subjectivity appears [viz., a conception of particulars as particulars]. Further, on account of the perfuming power of subjectivity, various modes of individuation are produced. And by clinging to them, various deeds are done, and we suffer as the result miseries, mentally as well as bodily.

There are two senses in what we call "the perfuming power of the external world of subjectivity": (1) that which strengthens particularisation;[1] (2) that which strengthens attachment.

There are again two senses in what we call "the perfuming power of the subjective mind": (1) that

[1] The older translation has "subjectivity" instead of "particularisation." These two terms are synonymous and frequently interchanged in the later translation as well as in the older one.

which strengthens the fundamental activity-consciousness, whereby Arhats, Pratyekabuddhas and Bodhisattvas are subject to the miseries of birth and death;
(2) that which strengthens the phenomena-particularising-consciousness, whereby all common people
(*prthagjana*) are subject to the miseries of being fettered by prior deeds (*karma*).

There are also two senses in what we call "the
perfuming power of ignorance": (1) a fundamental
perfuming, in the sense that the activity-consciousness
is thereby actualised; (2) a perfuming of intellect and
affection, in the sense that the phenomena-particularising-consciousness is thereby actualised.

How are pure things constantly produced by perfuming?

Suchness perfumes ignorance, and in consequence
of this perfuming the mind involved in subjectivity is
caused to loathe the misery of birth and death[1] and
to seek after the blessing of Nirvâna. This longing
and loathing on the part of the subjective mind in
turn perfumes suchness. On account of this perfuming influence we are enabled to believe that we are in
possession within ourselves of suchness whose essential nature is pure and immaculate; and we also recognise that all phenomena in the world are nothing
but the illusory manifestation of the mind (*âlaya-
vijñâna*) and have no reality of their own. Since we

[1] Birth and death do not necessarily refer to our life only, but
in their widest sense to the phenomenal world.

thus rightly understand the truth, we can practise the means of liberation, can perform those actions which are in accordance [with the Dharma]. Neither do we particularise, nor cling to. By virtue of this discipline and habituation during the lapse of innumerable asamkhyeyakalpas,[1] we have ignorance annihilated.

As ignorance is thus annihilated, the mind [i. e., âlaya-vijñâna] is no more disturbed so as to be subject to individuation. As the mind is no more disturbed, the particularisation of the surrounding world is annihilated. When in this wise the principle and the condition of defilement, their products, and the mental disturbances are all annihilated, it is said that we attain to Nirvâna and that various spontaneous displays of activity are accomplished.[2]

[1] Literally, countless ages, but it has a technical meaning. Childer's Pali Dictionary, sub voce: "The term kalpa is given to certain vast periods or cycles of time, of which there are three, Mahâkalpa, Asamkhyeyakalpa and Antarakalpa. All the Cakravâtas are subject to an alternate process of destruction and renovation, and a Mahâkalpa is a period which elapses from the commencement of a cakravâta to its complete destruction. Each Mahâkalpa is subdivided into four Asamkhyeyakalpâs. . . . Each Asamkhyeyakalpa contains twenty Antarakalpâs, an Antarakalpa being the interval that elapses while the age of man increases from ten years to an asamkhyeya, and then decreases again to ten years; this period is of immense duration." See also the third Koçathâna (chapter) of the Abhidharmakoça by Vasubandhu.

[2] Notice that Nirvâna is not inactivity or nothingness as commonly supposed. It is, according to Açvaghosha, the annihilation

There are two senses in what we call "the perfuming of the subjective mind": (1) the perfuming of the phenomena-particularising-consciousness, whereby all common people (*prthagjana*), Çrâvakas, and Pratyekabuddhas are induced to loathe the misery of birth and death, and, each according to his own capacity, to step towards the most excellent knowledge (*bodhiparinishpatti*); (2) the perfuming of the ego (*manas*), whereby courageously making up their minds, Bodhisattvas unhesitatingly step towards and enter into Nirvâna, that has no fixed abode.

There are also two senses in what we call "the perfuming of suchness": (1) essence-perfuming, and (2) activity-perfuming.

The Essence-Perfuming.—Embracing in full from all eternity infinite spotless virtues (*anâçrava*) and incomprehensibly excellent spiritual states that can efficiently exercise an eternal and incessant influence upon all beings, suchness thereby perfumes the minds of all beings.[1]

In consequence of this perfuming power, they are caused to loathe the misery of birth and death, and to long for the blessing of Nirvâna, and believing that they are in possession within themselves of the true,

of the ego-conception, freedom from subjectivity, insight into the essence of suchness, or the recognition of the oneness of existence.

[1] The older translation: "(1) Embracing from all eternity things spotless and possessing in full some inconceivable activity and (2) being capable to objectify itself, suchness through these two attributes constantly and eternally exercises its perfuming power."

valid Dharma, to call forth their aspiration (*cittotpâda*)[1] and to discipline themselves.

Here a question arises: If all beings are uniformly in possession of suchness and are therefore equally perfumed by it, how is it that there are some who do not believe in it, while others do; and that there are such immeasurable stages and inequalities among them, which divide the path from the first stage of aspiration up to the last stage of Nirvâna, while according to the Doctrine all these differences should be equalised?

In reply we say this: Though all beings are uniformly in possession of suchness, the intensity [of the influence] of ignorance, the principle of individuation, that works from all eternity, varies in such manifold grades as to outnumber the sands of the Ganges. And it is even so with such entangling prejudices (*kleça* or *âçrava*) as the ego-conception, intellectual and affectional prejudices, etc. [whose perfuming efficiency varies according to the karma previously accumulated by each individual],—all these things being comprehended only by the Tathâgata. Hence such immeasurable degrees of difference as regards belief, etc.[2]

[1] This has a technical sense and is explained below.

[2] The view here set forth is illustrated in the fifth chapter of the *Saddharma-pundarîka Sûtra* by the relation of the rain and plants. "Then, Kâçyapa, the grasses, shrubs, herbs, and wild trees in this universe, such as have young and tender stalks, twigs, leaves, and foliage, and such as have middle-sized stalks, twigs, leaves, and foliage, and such as have the same fully developed, all those grasses, shrubs, herbs, and wild trees, smaller and greater

Further, there is made in the doctrine of all Buddhas a distinction between *raison d'être* (*hetu*) and cause (*pratyaya*). When both are fully satisfied, the final goal [of Buddhism] is attained and actualised.

To illustrate: the combustible nature of the wood is the *raison d'être* of a fire. But if a man is not acquainted with the fact, or, though acquainted with it, does not apply any method [whereby the potential principle can be actualised], how could he produce a fire and burn the wood?

It is even so with all beings. Although they are in possession of suchness as the perfuming *raison d'être*, yet how could they attain to Nirvâna, if they do not happen, as the cause, to see Buddhas or Bodhisattvas, or good sages, or even if they see them, do not practise good deeds (*caryâ*), do not exercise wisdom (*prajñâ*), do not destroy prejudices (*kleça*)?

Conversely, by the cause alone, i. e., by their mere happening to see all good sages, it is not sure for them that they will be induced to loathe the misery

(other) trees will each, according to its faculty and power, suck the humid element from the water emitted by that great cloud, and by that water which, *all of one essence*, has been abundantly poured down by the cloud, they will each, according to its germ [i. e., karma], acquire a regular development, growth, shooting up, and bigness; and they will produce blossoms and fruits, and will receive, *each severally*, their names. Rooted in *one and the same* soil, *all those* [*different*] *families* of plants and germs are drenched and vivified by water *of one essence throughout*.'¹ (Kern's English Translation, p. 119. The italics and words in brackets are by the present translator.)

of birth and death and to long for the blessing of Nirvâna, unless indeed they were in possession within
themselves of the intrinsic perfuming principle as the
raison d'être. It is, therefore, only when both the
raison d'être and the cause are fully actualised that
they can do so.

How are the *raison d'être* and the cause to be fully
actualised?

Now, there is an inherent perfuming principle in
one's own being, which, embraced and protected by
the love (*maitrî*) and compassion (*karunâ*) of all Buddhas and Bodhisattvas, is caused to loathe the misery
of birth and death, to believe in Nirvâna, to cultivate
their root of merit (*kuçalamûla*), to habituate oneself
to it, and to bring it to maturity.

In consequence of this, one is enabled to see all
Buddhas and Bodhisattvas, and, receiving instructions from them, is benefited, gladdened, induced to
practise good deeds, etc., till one attain to Buddhahood and enter into Nirvâna.

The Activity-Perfuming.—By this is meant nothing
else than the perfuming influence of the external cause
over all beings. It asserts itself in innumerable ways.
Briefly speaking we may distinguish two kinds of it:
(1) individual; and (2) universal.

The Individual Cause.—All beings since their first
aspiration (*cittotpâda*) till the attainment of Buddhahood are sheltered under the guardianship of all Buddhas and Bodhisattvas who, responding to the re-

quirements of the occasion, transform themselves and
assume the actual forms of personality.

Thus for the sake of all beings Buddhas and Bodhisattvas become sometimes their parents, sometimes
their wives and children, sometimes their kinsmen,
sometimes their servants, sometimes their friends,
sometimes their enemies, sometimes reveal themselves as devas or in some other forms.

Again Buddhas and Bodhisattvas treat all beings
sometimes with the four methods of entertainment,[1]
sometimes with the six pâramitâs,[2] or with some other
deeds, all of which are the inducement for them to
make their knowledge (*bodhi*) perfect.

Thus embracing all beings with their deep compassion (*mahâkarunâ*), with their meek and tender
heart, as well as their immense treasure of blissful
wisdom, Buddhas convert them in such a way as to
suit their [all beings'] needs and conditions; while
all beings thereby are enabled to hear or to see Buddhas, and, thinking of Tathâgatas or some other per-
sonages, to increase their root of merit (*kuçalamûla*).

This individual cause is divided into two kinds:
(1) that which takes effect immediately, enabling one
without delay to attain to Buddhahood; (2) that which
takes effect gradually, enabling one to attain to Buddhahood only after a long interval.

[1] *Catvâri-sangrahavastûni* in Sanskrit.   They are (1) *dâna*,
charity; (2) *priyavacana*, endearing speech; (3) *arthacaryâ*, beneficial action; (4) *samânârthâ*, co-operation.

[2] This is explained below.

Each of these two is further divided into two kinds: (1) that which increases one's root of merit; (2) that which induces one to enter into the path (*mârga*).

The Universal Cause. — With universal wisdom (*samatâjñâna?*) and universal wishes (*samatâpranidhâna?*) all Buddhas and Bodhisattvas desire to achieve a universal emancipation of all beings. This desire is eternal and spontaneous on their part. And now as this wisdom and these wishes have the perfuming power over all beings, the latter are caused to think of or to recollect all Buddhas and Bodhisattvas, so that sometimes hearing them, sometimes seeing them, all beings thereby acquire [spiritual] benefits (*hitatâ*). That is, entering into the samâdhi of purity, they destroy hindrances wherever they are met with, and obtain all-penetrating insight,[1] that enables one to become conscious of the absolute oneness (*samatâ*) of the universe (*sarvaloka*) and to see innumerable Buddhas and Bodhisattvas.[2]

Again, this perfuming of the essence and the activity may be divided into two categories: (1) that which is not yet in unison [with suchness]; (2) that which is already in unison [with suchness].

By that perfuming which is not yet in unison [with suchness] we understand the religious discipline of

[1] Literally, an unimpeded eye.

[2] The older translation differs a little, but without any considerable change in the meaning.

common people (*prthagjana*), Çrâvakas, Pratyekabuddhas, and novice Bodhisattvas. While their
strength of faith (*çraddhâbala*) perfumed by the ego
(*manas*) and the ego-consciousness (*manovijñâna*) enables them to continue their religious discipline, they
have not yet attained to the state of non-particularisation, because their discipline is not yet in unison
with the essence of suchness ; nor have they yet attained to the spontaneity of action (*svayamkarma?*)[1],
because their discipline is not yet in unison with the
activity of suchness.

By that perfuming which is already in unison [with
suchness], we understand the religious discipline of
Bodhisattvas of the Dharmakâya. They have attended
to the state of non-particularisation, because their
discipline is in unison with the self-essence of all Tathâgatas ; they have attained to the spontaneity of action, because their discipline is in unison with the
wisdom and activity of all Tathâgatas. Allowing them-

---

[1] The spontaneity of action means action without attachment
or free from the ego-conception. It is somewhat similar to Lao-
Tze's idea of *wu wei*, non-assertion. Cf. also the following passages from the *Bhagavadgîtâ*, Chap. IV., p. 59 : "Actions defile
me not. I have no attachment to the fruit of actions." P. 60 :
"He is wise among men, he is possessed of devotion, who sees inaction in action and action in inaction." . . . "Forsaking all attachment to the fruit of action, always contented, dependent on
none, he does nothing at all, though he engages in action." P. 64 :
"He . . . who identifies his self with every being, is not tainted
though he performs (action)." "Action in inaction and inaction in
action " exactly coincides with the practical side of Açvaghosha's
doctrine of suchness (*bhûtatathatâ*).

selves to be influenced only by the power of the Dharma, their discipline acquires a nature of spontaneity and thereby perfumes suchness and destroys ignorance.

Again the incessant perfuming of the defiled dharma [i. e., ignorance] from all eternity works on; but when one attains to Buddhahood, one at once puts an end to it.

The perfuming of the pure dharma [i. e., suchness] works on to eternity, and there is no interruption of it. Because by virtue of the perfuming of the Dharma, that is, suchness, subjectivity is on the one hand annihilated, and the Dharmakâya is on the other hand revealed, and the perfuming process of the activity [of suchness] thus originated forever goes on.

c. The Threefold Significance of the Mahâyâna Explained.

Again the quintessence and the attributes of suchness (*bhûtatathatâ*) know no diminution or addition, but remain the same in common people (*prthagjana*), Çrâvakas, Pratyekabuddhas, Bodhisattvas, and Buddhas. It was not created in the past, nor is it to be annihilated in the future; it is eternal, permanent, absolute ; and from all eternity it sufficingly embraces in its essence all possible merits (*punya*).

That is to say, suchness has such characteristics as follows : the effulgence of great wisdom ; the universal illumination of the dharmadhâtu [universe]; the true and adequate knowledge ; the mind pure and

clean in its self-nature; the eternal, the blessed, the
self-regulating and the pure;[1] the tranquil, the immutable, and the free.   And there is no heterogeneity
in all those Buddha-dharmas which, outnumbering
the sands of the Ganges, can be neither identical
(*ekârtha*) nor not-identical (*nânârtha*) [with the essence
of suchness], and which therefore are out of the range
of our comprehension. Accordingly suchness is called
the Tathâgata's womb (*tathâgatagarbha*) or the Dharmakâya.[2]

It may be questioned: While it was stated before
that suchness is devoid of all characteristics (*lakshana*),
how can it now be said without contradiction that it
embraces in full all such merits?

In reply it would be said that though suchness in
truth abundantly embraces all merits, yet it is free in
its nature from all forms of distinction; because all
objects in the world are of one and the same taste,
are of one reality, have nothing to do with the modes
of particularisation, and are not of dualistic character.
Depending on the principle of birth-and-death, such
as the activity-consciousness (*karmavijñâna?*), etc.,
however, all signs of difference and individuation appear.

[1] These four qualities are usually considered by Mahâyânists
to be those of Nirvâna as well.

[2] Observe here again that Dharmakâya is used in a sense quite
different from its ordinary interpretation as the "Body of the
Law."

How are those qualifications to be assigned to suchness?

Though all things in their [metaphysical] origin come from the soul alone and in truth free from particularisation, yet on account of non-enlightenment there originates a subjective mind [i. e., *âlaya-vijñâna*] that becomes conscious of an external world (*vishaya*). This we call ignorance (*avidya*). Nevertheless the essence of the mind [or the soul] is perfectly pure, and there is no awakening of ignorance in it. Thence we assign to suchness this quality, the effulgence of great wisdom.

If the mind being awakened perceive an external world, then there will be something that cannot be perceived by it. But the essence of the mind has nothing to do with perception [which presupposes the dual existence of a perceiving subject and an object perceived]; so there is nothing that cannot be perceived by it, [that is, the world of relativity is submerged in the oneness of suchness]. Thence we assign to suchness this quality, the universal illumination of the universe (*dharmadhâtu*).

When the mind is disturbed, it fails to be a true and adequate knowledge ; it fails to be a pure, clean essence ; it fails to be eternal, blissful, self-regulating, and pure ; it fails to be tranquil, etc. On the contrary, it will become transient, changeable, unfree, and therefore the source of falsity and defilement, while its modifications outnumber the sands of the

Ganges.   But when there is no disturbance in the
essence of the mind, we speak of suchness as being
the true, adequate knowledge, etc., and as possessing
pure and clean merits that outnumber the sands of
the Ganges.

When the mind is disturbed it will strive to become conscious of the existence of an external world
and will thus betray the imperfection of its inner
condition. But as all infinite merits in fact constitute
the one mind which, perfect in itself, has no need of
seeking after any external things other than itself, so
suchness never fails to actualise all those Buddha-
dharmas, that, outnumbering the sands of the Ganges,
can be said to be neither identical nor non-identical
with the essence of the mind, and that therefore are
utterly out of the range of our comprehension.   On
that account suchness is designated the Tathâgata's
womb (*tathâgatagarbha*) or the Tathâgata's Dharmakâya.

What is meant by the activity of suchness is this:
all Buddhas, while at the stage of discipline, feel a
deep compassion (*mahâkarunâ*) [for all beings], practise all pâramitâs, the four methods of entertainment
(*catvâri-sangrahavastûni*), and many other meritorious
deeds; treat others as their own self, wish to work
out a universal salvation of mankind in ages to come,
through limitless numbers of kalpas; recognise truthfully and adequately the principle of equality (*samatâ*)

among people; and do not cling to the individual existence of a sentient being.[1]

By virtue of such a great wisdom that works means
of emancipation (*upâyajñâ?*),[2] they annihilate ignorance that knows no beginning; recognise the Dharmakâya in its original purity; spontaneously perform incomprehensible karma[3] as well as various unfettered
moral activities; manifest themselves throughout the
universe (*dharmadhâtu*), identify themselves with
suchness, and leave no traces of compulsion.[4]

And how is this?

Because all Tathâgatas are the Dharmakâya itself,[5] are the highest truth (*paramârthasatya*) itself,

[1] The older translation reads: "For they consider all sentient
beings as their own self and do not cling to their individual forms.
How is this? Because they know truthfully that all sentient beings as well as their own self come from one and the same suchness, and no distinction can be established among them."

[2] Cf. the second, third, fourth, fifth, and seventh chapter of
the *Saddharma-pundarîka Sûtra*, in which Buddha preaches
about the means of salvation.

[3] That is, "action in inaction and inaction in action."

[4] Açvaghosha's conception of religious life as identical in its
essence with poetry or fine art, I think, closely resembles that of
Kant who says in his *Critique of Judgment* that the production
of fine art should appear as if the work of nature. To quote his
own words: "Als Natur aber erscheint ein Produkt der Kunst da-
durch, dass zwar alle Pünktlichkeit in der Uebereinkunft mit Re-
geln, nach denen allein das Produkt das werden kann, was es sein
soll, angetroffen wird, aber ohne Peinlichkeit, d. i., ohne eine Spur
zu zeigen, dass die Regel dem Künstler vor Augen geschwebt und
seinen Gemüthskräften Fesseln angelegt habe." (*Kritik der Ur-
theilskraft*, Kirchmann's edition, p. 169.)

[5] Cf. *Vajracchedikâ*, Chap. XVII: "And why, O Subhûti, the

and have nothing to do with conditionality (*samvrtti-satya*) and compulsory actions; whereas the seeing, hearing, etc. [i. e., the particularising senses] of the sentient being diversify [on its own account] the activity of Tathâgatas.

Now this activity [in another word, the Dharma-kâya] has a twofold aspect. The first one depends on the phenomena-particularising-consciousness, by means of which the activity is conceived by the minds of common people (*prthagjana*), Çrâvakas, and Prat-yekabuddhas. This aspect is called the Body of Transformation (*nirmânakâya*).

But as the beings of this class do not know that the Body of Transformation is merely the shadow [or reflection] of their own evolving-consciousness (*pra-vrtti-vijñâna*), they imagine that it comes from some external sources, and so they give it a corporeal limitation. But the Body of Transformation [or what amounts to the same thing, the Dharmakâya] has nothing to do with limitation and measurement.[1]

The second aspect [of the Dharmakâya] depends on the activity-consciousness (*karmavijñâna*) by means of which the activity is conceived by the minds of

name of Tathâgata? It expresses true suchness (*bhûtatathatâ*). . . . It expresses that he had no origin. . . . It expresses the destruction of all qualities (*dharma*). . . . It expresses one who had no origin whatever. . . . Because, O Subhûti, no-origin is the highest goal."

[1] The older translation reads simply: "They cannot thoroughly understand it [i. e., the true nature of the *Nirmânakâya*.]"

Bodhisattvas while passing from their first aspiration (*cittotpâda*) stage up to the height of Bodhisattva-hood. This is called the Body of Bliss (*sambhoga-kâya*).

The body has infinite forms. The form has infinite attributes. The attribute has infinite excellencies. And the accompanying rewards[1] of Bodhisattvas, that is, the region where they are predestined to be born [by their previous karma], also has infinite merits and ornamentations. Manifesting itself everywhere, the Body of Bliss is infinite, boundless, limitless, un-intermittent [in its action], directly coming forth from the mind.[2]

All these merits being actualised through the per-fuming of such spotless deeds as the pâramitâs[3], etc., as well as through the incomprehensible perfuming power [of enlightenment *a priori*], the Sambhogakâya

[1] Buddhists distinguish two kinds of the retribution which we receive as the fruit of karma previously accumulated by ourselves: the first one called "principal" is our bodily existence; the second called "accompanying" is the region where we are destined to be born.

[2] The older translation has: "It is boundless, cannot be ex-hausted, is free from the signs of limitation. Manifesting itself wherever it should manifest itself, it always exists by itself and is never destroyed or lost."

[3] The six Pâramitâs are commonly enumerated: (1) charity (*dâna*); (2) morality (*çîla*); (3) patience (*ksânti*); (4) energy (*vîrya*); (5) meditation (*dhyâna*); (6) wisdom (*prajñâ*). When we speak of the ten Pâramitâs, the following four are to be added: expediency (*upâya*); prayer or vow (*pranidhâna*); strength (*bala*); knowledge (*jnâna*). An explanation of the six Pâramitâs is given below.

embraces infinite attributes of bliss and merit. Therefore it is also called the Body of Reward.

What is recognised by common people (*prthagjana*), etc., is the coarsest form of the activity of the
Dharmakâya. There is a variety of it according to
the six different states of creation.[1] It has no attributes of infinite merits and blessings.

What is recognised by Bodhisattvas at the first
stage is a finer form of the activity of the Dharmakâya. As they firmly believe in suchness, they can
have a partial insight into it, and understand that the
Body of the Tathâgata is not departing, is not coming, is free from arrest[2] [i. e., the Tathâgata's work
is eternal and constant], that every thing is but a reflected shadow of the mind, not independent of suchness. But these Bodhisattvas have not yet freed
themselves from the finest form of particularisation,
because they have not yet entered into the order of
the Dharmakâya.

Bodhisattvas at the stage of pure-heartedness are
able to recognise the finer form of the activity [of the
Dharmakâya]. Their insight is more penetrating than
the former. When they reach the height of Bodhisattvahood their insight becomes perfect.

By the finer form of the activity we understand

[1] The six states of creation (*gati*) are: (1) *Deva* (gods); (2)
Manushya (men); (3) *Asura* (demons); (4) *Preta* (ghosts); (5) *Tiryagyoni* (animals); (6) *Nâraka* (inhabitants of hell).

[2] Cf. the *Vajracchedikâ Sûtra*, Chap. XXIX (*Sacred Books
of the East*, Vol. XLIX., p. 142).

the Body of Bliss (*sambhogakâya*). As long as they are possessed by the activity-consciousness, they would conceive the Body of Bliss.[1] But when they are liberated from it, all traces of individuation would become obliterated. Because all Tathâgatas come from [one and the same] Dharmakâya, have no distinction of this-ness and that-ness, have no corporeal forms that are characterised by reciprocal limitation.

A question arises here: If the Dharmakâya of Buddhas is devoid of variously differentiated corporeal forms, how is it that it can manifest itself in various corporeal forms at all?

In reply we say: The Dharmakâya can manifest itself in various corporeal forms just because it is the real essence of them. Matter (*rûpa*) and mind (*citta*) from the very beginning are not a duality. So we speak of [the universe as] a system of rationality (*prajñakâya*), seeing that the real nature of matter just constitutes the norm of mind. Again we speak of [the universe as] a system of materiality (*dharmakâya*), seeing that the true nature of mind just constitutes the norm of matter.[2]

Now depending on the Dharmakâya, all Tathâgatas manifest themselves in bodily forms and are inces-

[1] The last two sentences are missing in the older translation.

[2] Cf. the following passages from the *Prajñâ-pâramitâ-hrdaya Sûtra*: "Form (*rûpa*) is emptiness (*çûnyatâ*), and emptiness is indeed form. Emptiness is not different from form, form is not different from emptiness. What is form that is emptiness, what is emptiness that is form."

santly present at all points of space.[1] And Bodhisattvas in the ten quarters, according to their capabilities
and wishes, are able to manifest infinite Bodies of
Bliss and infinite lands of ornamentation, each one of
which, though stamped with the marks of individuality, does not hinder the others from being fused into
it, and this [mutual fusion] has no interruption.

But the manifestation of the Dharmakâya in [in-
finite] bodily forms is not comprehensible to the
thought and understanding of common people; because it is the free and subtlest activity of suchness.[2]

Again, in order that all beings might be induced
to step forward from the gate of birth-and-death to
that of suchness, we endeavor to let them understand
that those modes of existence such as matter (*rûpa*),
etc. [i. e., the five skandhas][3] are imperfect.

Why are they imperfect?

When we divide some gross [or composite] matter, we can reduce it to atoms (*anu*). But as the atom
will also be subject to further division, all forms of
material existence, whether gross or fine, are nothing
but the shadow of particularisation produced by a
subjective mind, and we cannot ascribe any degree of
[absolute, or independent] reality to them.

[1] The older translation: "Therefore it is preached that the
Dharmakâya is omnipresent. The corporeal forms by which it
manifests itself have no limitation."

[2] This passage is missing in the older translation.

[3] They are matter (*rûpa*); sensation (*vedanâ*); idea (*samjnâ*);
action (*samskâra*); and consciousness (*vijnâna*).

Let us next go over to and examine the other skandhas [that have temporal existence]. We find there too that we can gradually reduce them to kshanas [i. e., infinitesimal divisions of time], whose nature, however closely scrutinised, does not give any sign of [indivisible] oneness.

It is even the same with the objects of non-aggregate (*asamskrta-dharma*).[1] They cannot have their own existence independent of the universe (*dharmadhâtu*). Be it therefore understood that the same may be said in regard to all objects without exception in the ten quarters of space.[2]

As a lost man who takes the east for the west,

[1] All phenomena in the world, physical as well as mental, are divided into two great classes : (1) *Samskrtadharma*, i. e., that which consists of parts temporal or spatial; (2) *Asamskrtadharma*, i. e., that which does not consist of parts. The first class is subdivided into four principal departments which are also subject to a further subdivision, seventy-two in the Hînayâna system (according to the *Abhidharmakoça-çâstra*), and ninety-four in the Mahâyâna (according to the *Vijnânamâtrasiddhi-çâstra*). The four principal departments are : (1) *Rûpa* (physical phenomena); (2) *Citta* (thought or understanding); (3) *Caittadharma* or *Cittasamprayuktasamskâra* (mental phenomena); (4) *Cittaviprayuktasamskâra* (that which does not belong to the former, namely, relation that obtains among things). As for the second class, *Asamskrtadharma*, Mahâyânists subdivide it into six while Hînayânists subdivide it into three. For details see the two Çâstras above mentioned.

[2] The last five paragraphs are missing in the older translation which has simply this instead: "The external world which consists in the six objects of sense does not exist independently of our mind, and the mind having no forms and attributes cannot be grasped even if we search for it throughout the ten quarters."

while the quarter is not changed on account of his confusion, so all beings, because of their misleading ignorance, imagine that the mind is being disturbed, while in reality it is not.

But when they understand that the disturbance of the mind [i. e., birth-and-death] is [at the same time] immortality [viz., suchness], they would then enter into the gate of suchness.

2. The Refutation of False Doctrines.

All false doctrines invariably come out of the âtman-conception. If we were liberated from it, the existence of false doctrines would be impossible.

There are two kinds of the âtman-conception: (1) Belief in the existence of a personal âtman [or ego-soul]; (2) Belief in the existence of âtman in things [or things-in-themselves].[1]

a. Five False Views Held by Those Who Believe in a Personal Atman.

There are five different views springing from it [belief in the ego], which are held by common people (prthagjana).

First, hearing that it is said in the Sûtra[2] that the

[1] This denial of the existence of things-in-themselves is one of the principal features of the Mahâyâna as distinguished from the Hînayâna Buddhism.

[2] It is not exactly known to what Sûtra or Sûtras this refers, but the analogy of this kind is frequently met with in most of the Mahâyâna texts.

Dharmakâya of the Tathâgata is perfectly tranquil and may be likened unto space (*âkâsa*), yet not understanding its purport, ignorant people cling to the view that the nature of the Tathâgata is eternal and omnipresent in the same sense as space is.

In order that this clinging to the false doctrine may be eliminated, be it clearly understood that space is nothing but a mode of particularisation and that it has no real existence of its own. Where there is a perception of space, there is side by side a perception of a variety of things, in contradistinction to which space is spoken of as if existing independently. Space therefore exists only in relation to our particularising consciousness.

Further since matter (*rûpa*) as stated before, is merely a particularisation of the confused mind, it is clear enough that space cannot have any independent existence. In a word all modes of relative existence, our phenomenal world as a whole, are created simply by the particularisation of the confused mind. If we become dissociated from the latter, then all modes of relative existence vanish away by themselves ; while the soul alone, in its truth and suchness, pervades the whole universe. The soul, therefore, that constitutes the essential nature of the Tathâgata, cannot be compared with space, though the latter may be said to be in a certain limited sense eternal and real.

Secondly, hearing that it is said in the Sûtras that all things in the world without exception are perfect emptiness (*atyantaçûnyatâ*), that even Nirvâna[1] or suchness is also perfect emptiness, is devoid in its true nature of all characteristics (*lakshanâ*), yet not understanding its purport, ignorant people cling to the view that Nirvâna or suchness is a nothing, devoid of contents.

In order that this clinging may be eliminated, be it clearly understood that suchness or Dharmakâya in its self-nature (*svabhâva*) is not a nothing (*çûnyatâ*) but envelopes in full immeasurable merits (*guna*) which make up its true nature.

Thirdly, hearing that it is said in the Sûtras[2] that the Tathâgata's womb (*tathâgatagarbha*) envelopes in full all kinds of merits which constituting its true nature do neither suffer augmentation nor diminution, yet not understanding its purport, ignorant people cling to the view that there is in the Tathâgata's womb itself an inherent and fundamental distinction between the two objects, matter (*rûpa*) and mind (*citta*).

In order that this clinging may be eliminated, be

---

[1] Fa-tsang, a commentator of the present Discourse, quotes the *Mahâprajnâ-pâramitâ-Sûtra* as here referred to. The Sûtra says : "Even Nirvâna is like a mirage, like a dream. Nay, if there be something superior to Nirvâna, I declare it is also like a mirage, like a dream."

[2] For instance, we read in the second volume of the *Lankâvatara Sûtra* (translated into Chinese by Çiksânanda): "The Tathâgatagarbha is in its intrinsic nature pure, clean, eternal, permanent, unintermittent, and immutable; it embraces the thirty-two excellent qualities, and abides within the body of all sentient beings," etc.

it clearly understood that suchness (*bhûtatathatâ*) has nothing to do with any form of distinction produced by defilement, and that even in case we speak of its possessing innumerable meritorious characteristics, they are free from the traces of defilement.

Fourthly, hearing that it is said in the Sûtras[1] that even all impure and defiled things in the world are produced through the Tathâgata's womb (*tathâgata-garbha*), and that all things in the world are not at variance with suchness, yet not understanding its purport, ignorant people imagine that the Tathâgata's womb all-containingly envelopes all objects of defilement in the world.

In order that this clinging may be eliminated, be it clearly understood that the Tathâgata's womb all-containingly envelopes pure and spotless merits (*guna*) which, outnumbering the sands of the Ganges, are not at variance with suchness; that the prejudices (*âçrava* or *kleça*) and defiled objects, which also outnumber the sands of the Ganges are nothing but non-entity, have from the first no self-existence (*svabhâva*), have never been in correspondence with the Tathâgata's womb; that there is no reason to suppose that the Tathâgata's womb had been corresponding with defiled objects, but has now by virtue of intellectual intuition been freed from falsity and defilement.

[1] Though not exactly known to what Sûtra or Sûtras the reference is made here, we can easily find similar passages in the Mahâyâna texts, such as the *Lankâvatara*, the *Crîmâlâ*, etc.

Fifthly, hearing that it is said in the Sûtras[1] that
depending on the Tathâgata's womb, there is birth-
and-death (*samsâra*) as well as the attainment of Nirvâna, yet not understanding its purport, ignorant people imagine that depending on the Tathâgata's womb
there is a beginning for birth-and-death, and that
since there is the beginning, Nirvâna is in turn subject to extinction.

In order that this clinging may be eliminated, be
it clearly understood that as the Tathâgata's womb
has no beginning, ignorance and birth-and-death depending on it have also no beginning ; that it is a view
held by the tîrthaka[2] [i. e., the followers of the Vaiçe-

---

[1] These are not also exactly known.

[2] It is not precisely known how many philosophical schools,
called tîrthakas by Buddhists, were flourishing just at the time
of Açvaghosha. The *Nirvâna Sûtra* and the *Vimalakîrttinir-
deça Sûtra* mention six of them which were existing at the time
of Buddha: (1) Pûrana Kâçyapa; (2) Maskarin Goçâliputra; (3)
Sañjayin Vairaṭṭîputra; (4) Ajita Keçakambala; (5) Kakuda Kâtyâyana; (6) Nirgrantha Jñâtiputra. In a commentary on the *Vi-
jñânamâtrâ-çâstra*, however, which is a later production than this
Discourse, twelve different tîrthaka schools are enumerated. They
are: (1) the Samkhya school; (2) the Vaiçesika school; (3) the
school which believes in Maheçvara as the creator; (4) the school
which believes in Mahâbrahma as the creator; (5) the school
which maintains that Time is the creator; (6) the school which
maintains that Space is the creator; (7) the school which maintains
that Water is the creator; (8) the school which says that the world
exists by itself; (9) the school which says that the creation comes
from Quarters; (10) the school which maintains that the Ego is
the principle of existence; (11) the school which maintains the immortality of articulate sounds, i. e., the Mîmamsâ school; (12) the
Lokâyatika school, an Indian materialism. For further references

sika] and not taught by the Buddha, to say that there
are outside of the three worlds[1] (*triloka*) some other
beings coming into existence; that the Tathâgata's
womb has no future [i. e., time of extinction]; and
that those who have an insight into it, will eternally
destroy the seeds of birth-and-death and attain to
Nirvâna which has also no future [i. e.; time of extinc-
tion].

These four[2] erroneous views have thus arisen from
the conception of a personal âtman, and so we have
laid down the four refutations as above mentioned.[3]

b. *Belief in the Existence of Atman in Things.*

As the World-honored One (*Bhagavat*), consider-
ing the inferior intellectual calibre of Çrâvakas and
Pratyekabuddhas, taught them only the doctrine of
non-personal âtman, [and did not make any further

see Dr. Enryô Inouye's *Gedô Tetsugaku* (*Philosophical Systems
of the Tîrthakas*), 1897, Tokyo, Japan.

[1] They are the world of desire (*kâmaloka*), the world of form
(*rûpaloka*), the world of formlessness (*arûpaloka*). (See also p.
77). The *kâmaloka* is divided into hells (*naraka*), region of ghosts
(*preta*), animal life (*tiryagyoni*), human life (*manushyaloka*), and
region of gods (*deva*); the *rûpaloka* into 17 heavenly abodes corresponding to the three stages of Dhyâna; the *arûpaloka* into four
heavenly abodes. For details see the second chapter of the *Abhidharmakoça-Çâstra*, by Vasubandhu.

[2] The number "four" in this paragraph should be "five," for
the author enumerates five misunderstandings and their refutations, as we have seen.

[3] The whole passage is missing in the older translation.

demonstration of the doctrine], the people have in the meantime formed a fixed idea on the transitoriness of the five skandhas,[1] and, being terrified at the thought of birth and death, have fanatically craved for Nirvâna.

In order that this clinging may be eliminated, be it clearly understood that the essence of the five skandhas is uncreate, there is no annihilation of them ; that since there is no annihilation of them, they are in their [metaphysical] origin Nirvâna itself ; that if one be absolutely freed from particularisation and attachment, one will understand that all things both pure and defiled have only relative existence.

Be it therefore known that all things in the world from the beginning are neither matter (*rûpa*), nor mind (*citta*), nor intelligence (*prajñâ*), nor consciousness (*vijñâna*), nor non-being (*abhâva*), nor being (*bhâva*); they are after all inexplicable. The reason why the Tathâgata nevertheless endeavors to instruct by means of words and definitions is through his good and excellent skilfulness [or expediency, *upâya-kauçalya*].[2] He only provisionally makes use of words and definitions to lead all beings, while his real object is to make them abandon symbolism and directly enter

[1] See p. 104, footnote.

[2] See the second chapter of the *Saddarmapundarîka Sûtra*, in which Buddha teaches how the only one yâna (vehicle) is split through his transcendental upâya (skilfulness or expediency) into three yânas : Çrâvakayâna, Pratyekabuddhayâna, and Bodhisattvayâna.

into the real reality (*tattva*). Because if they indulge themselves in reasonings, attach themselves to sophistry, and thus foster their subjective particularisation, how could they have the true wisdom (*tattvajñâna*) and attain to Nirvâna?

3. Ways of Practising the Right Path.

By this we mean that all Bodhisattvas, by their aspiration (*cittotpâda*)[1] and discipline (*caryâcarana*), will be able to attain to the reason that made all Tathâgatas perceive the path (*mârga*).

Briefly stated, there are three kinds of aspiration: (1) Aspiration through the perfection of faith; (2) Aspiration through knowledge and practice; (3) Aspiration through intellectual intuition.

By whom, and by which deeds, can faith (*çraddhâ*) be perfected and can the aspiration be awakened?

Now the people who belong to the group of incon-

---

[1]Aspiration which does not exactly correspond to the Chinese *fah hsin* and Sanskrit *cittotpâda*, has been retained for lack of a fitter term. It has a technical sense in Buddhism. Literally, *fah* or *utpâda* means producing, raising, or awakening, while *hsin* or *citta* as noticed elsewhere is mind, thought, or consciousness. *Cittopâda*, however, is more than the raising of one's thought to a higher religious life; it means the recognition of the truth that one is in possession within oneself of the highest perfect knowledge (*samyaksambodhi*); it is the birth within oneself of a higher ethical impulse constituting the essence of religion. A fuller form of *fah hsin* is *fah bodhi hsin* or *fah anuttarasamyaksambodhi hsin*. See the Mahâyâna Sûtras such as the *Saddharma Pundarîka*, *Vajracchedikâ*, *Sukhâvati Vyuha*, *Lankâvatara*, *Avatamsaka*, etc.

stancy (*aniyatarâçi*),[1] by virtue of their root of merit (*kuçalamûla*), which has a perfuming power, firmly believe in the retribution of karma, practise the ten virtues (*daçakuçalâni*),[2] loathe the sufferings of birth and death, seek after the most excellent enlightenment (*Samyaksambodhi*), and seeing Buddhas and Bodhisattvas they wait on them, make offerings to them, discipline themselves in many [meritorious] deeds ; and after the lapse of ten thousand kalpas (eons), their faith will finally be perfected.

Since then either by virtue of the instruction received from Buddhas and Bodhisattvas, or on account of their deep compassion (*mahâkarunâ*), or from their desire to preserve the right doctrine (*saddharma*) against its corruption, their aspiration [to the highest truth] will be awakened.

After having awakened the aspiration they will

---

[1] There are three groups of people : (1) Those who are constantly abiding in absolute truth (*samyaktvaniyata-râçi*) ; (2) Those who are constantly abiding in falsehood (*mithyâtvaniyata-râçi*) ; (3) Those who are inconstant (*aniyata-râçi*).

[2] The ten virtues (*daçakuçalâni*) consist in not committing the ten evils (*daçâkuçalâni*) which are as follows : (1) Killing a living being (*prânâtipâda*) ; (2) Stealing (*adattâdâna*) ; (3) Committing adultery (*kâmamithyâcâra*) ; (4) Lying (*mrshâvâda*) ; (5) Slander (*paiçunya*) ; (6) Insulting speech (*pârushya*) ; (7) Frivolous talk (*sambhinnapralâpa*) ; (8) Avarice (*abhidhya*) ; (9) Evil intent (*vyâpâda*); (10) False view (*mithyâdrshthi*). The ten evils here enumerated should be avoided by the lay members of Buddhism. For the Çramaneras there is a different set of precepts specially intended for them, called the *Daçaçikshapada*, with which the ten virtues must not be confused as they are by some.

enter into the group of constant truth (*samyaktvani-yata-râçi*) and never relapse, always abiding in the essence of the Buddha-seed and identifying themselves with its excellent principle.

There is, however, a certain class of people whose root of merit (*kuçalamûla*) from time immemorial is poor, and whose prejudices (*kleça* or *âçrava*) are intense, deeply veiling their minds. Such people, even if they see Buddhas and Bodhisattvas, wait on them, and make offerings to them, will sow merely the seeds of men (*manushya*) and gods (*deva*) [i. e., they will be born in the future as men or gods], or the seeds of the enlightenment of Çrâvakas and Pratyekabuddhas [i. e., their attainment would not be higher than that of Çrâvakas or Pratyekabuddhas].

Some of them may even aspire to seek after the Mahâbodhi,[1] but owing to the instability of their character, they will ever osciliate between progress and retrogression.

Some of them, happening to see Buddhas and Bodhisattvas, may make offerings to them, wait on them, practise many [meritorious] deeds, and, while ten thousand mahâkalpas (æons) are not yet elapsed, may meantime come into some favorable circumstances and thereby awake aspiration. What are those favorable circumstances? For instance, they may witness the personal figure of a Buddha, or may make some offerings to the congregation of priests

---

[1] The older translation reads "Mahâyâna."

(*samgha*), or may be instructed by Çrâvakas or Pratyekabuddhas, or may be moved by seeing others aspire [to the highest truth].

But this kind of aspiration as a rule is not constant. In case they come into unfavorable circumstances, they may happen to fall down to the stage of
Çrâvakahood or Pratyekabuddhahood.

Now, briefly speaking, three faculties of the soul
will be awakened by the perfection of faith : (1) right-
ness of comprehension [lit., right, straight mind], for
it truthfully and intuitively contemplates suchness
(*bhûtatathatâ*); (2) profundity of virtue [lit., deep,
heavy mind], for it rejoices in accumulating all good
deeds ; (3) greatness of compassion (*mahâkarunâ*), for
it desires to uproot the miseries (*duhkha*) of all beings.

It may be asked whether there is ever any need
for one to discipline oneself in all good deeds and to
try to save mankind, since all sentient beings (*sarvasattva*) as well as all things (*sarvadharma*) in the world,
abiding in the oneness of the universe (*dharmadhâtu*)
that has no second, will, as can be logically inferred,
have nothing to do but calmly to contemplate suchness.

In reply we say, yes. Because the mind may be
likened unto a precious jewel which is pure and bright
in its essence but buried in a gross veinstone. Now
there is no reason to suppose that one can make it
clean and pure only by contemplating it, and without

applying any means [of purification] or a degree of workmanship.

It is even the same with suchness. Though it is pure and bright in its essence and sufficiently envelopes all merits (*guna*), yet it is deeply buried in infinite external defilements. And there is no reason to suppose that a man can make it pure and clean only by earnest contemplation on it, and without trying any means [of emancipation] or of discipline.

It is therefore an urgent necessity that all good deeds should be accumulated, that all beings should be delivered, that those infinite external defilements and impurities should be cast off, that the true doctrine should be revealed.

With regard to "means" [or "skilfulness," *upâya*] there are, briefly stated, four kinds.

The first one is called the means of practising the fundamental [truth, *mûla*]. That is to say, by contemplating the true essence of all dharmas, which, being uncreate and free from imagination, is not concerned with the metempsychosis of birth and death, and by contemplating the truth that all things originate from the co-operation of the principle (*hetu*) and the causes (*pratyaya*), and that the retribution of karma is irrevocable, one will evoke deep compassion, discipline oneself in all good deeds, embrace and convert all beings, and not dwell in Nirvâna, since suchness [in its absolute aspect] has nothing to do with Nirvâna or with birth-and-death. As this attitude [towards all objects] is in accord [with the nature of suchness], it is called the means of practising the [fundamental] truth.

The second one is called the means of abeyance. That is, by feeling shame and remorse, one may put an end to all evils and not let them grow, since suchness is free from all marks of imperfection. Thus to be in accord with suchness and to put an end to all evils is called the means of abeyance.

The third one is called the means of strengthening the root of merits (*kuçalamûla*). By raising reverential feelings toward the Triple Treasure (*triratna*), one will revere, make offerings to, pay homage to, praise, rejoice in, and beseech the Triple Treasure; and thereupon one's orthodox faith being strengthened, one will at last awake a desire for the most excellent knowledge (*bodhiparinishpatti*). Through the protection of the majestic power of the Buddha, Dharma, and Samgha, one's karma-hindrances (*karmâvarana*) will now get purified and one's root of merit firmly established; because suchness is free from all hindrances and envelopes all merits. Thus to be in accord with suchness and to practise good deeds is called the means of strengthening the root of merits.

The fourth one is called the universal means of great vows (*mahâpranidhâna*). That is, one may make the vow that in ages to come all beings should universally be delivered and take refuge at ease in the

Anupadhiçesa Nirvâna,[1] because the true nature of all objects is free from relativity, is one and the same, making no distinction between this and that, and is absolutely calm and tranquil. Thus to be in accord with the three attributes [i. e., non-relativity, sameness, tranquillity] of suchness and to make such a great vow is called the universal means of great vows.

[Now to return to the former subject], when the Bodhisattva thus aspires to the highest truth, he is able to have a partial insight into the Dharmakâya of the Buddha ; and according to the power of the vow (*pranidhânavaça*), he performs eight things, to wit, his descent from the palace in the Tushita heaven[2]

---

[1] Mahâyânists in general distinguish four aspects of Nirvâna ; (1) Nirvâna that is pure and spotless in its self-nature, i. e., absolute suchness, possessed equally by all beings; (2) Nirvâna that has remnant (*upadhiçesa*), i. e., a state of relative suchness, which, though freed from the affectional hindrance (*kleçâvarana*), is still under the fetter of materiality, which causes suffering and misery; (3) Nirvâna that has no remnant (*anupadhiçesa*), i. e., a state of relative suchness which is free from the misery of birth and death, being entirely liberated from the fetter of materiality ; (4) Nirvâna that has no fixed abode, i. e., a state of suchness in its spontaneous activity which is free from the intellectual hindrance (*jneyâvarana*) and full of love and wisdom, believes neither in birth-and-death nor in Nirvâna, but eternally abiding in the suchness of things benefits all sentient beings. Çrâvakas and Pratyekabuddhas can recognise the first three aspects of Nirvâna, but the last one is known only to Buddhas and Bodhisattvas. For further details see the tenth volume of the *Vijnânamâtrasiddhi Çâstra*, translated into Chinese by Hüan-tsang.

[2] One of the six heavenly abodes of the *Kâmaloka* (world of desire). The heavenly abodes are: (1) Region of the four kings of the cardinal points (*mahârâjakâyika*) ; (2) that of the thirty-

[to this world], his entrance into the human womb, his stay therein, his birth, his renunciation, his attainment of Buddhahood, his revolution of the Dharma-wheel (*dharmacakra*), and lastly his Parinirvâna.

He is not, however, as yet to be called absolute Dharmakâya, for he has not yet completely destroyed the impure[1] karma that has been accumulated during his numberless existences in the past; perchance by the influence of the evil karma he may suffer a little amount of misery. But he suffers it only for a short time, and this not because of his being fettered by the evil karma, but because of his own vow-power (*pranidhânavaça*) [which he made for the universal emancipation of mankind].

It is sometimes said in the Sûtra[2] that even those Bodhisattvas who aspired[to the highest truth]through the perfection of their faith might relapse and fall down to the evil creation (*apâyagati*).[3] But this was

three gods (*trâyastrinça*); (3) the *Yâmâ*; (4) the *Tushita*; (5) the *Nirmânatis*; (6) the *Paranirmita-vaçavatins*. See also the note to Triloka, p. 77.

[1] The term *impure* does not mean immoral, but relative, conditional, dualistic or material, in contradistinction to pure, absolute, unconditional, spiritual, etc.

[2] For instance, it is stated in the second fasciculus of the *Bodhisattva-kusumamâlâ-pûrvakarma Sûtra* (? *P'u-sa ying-lo pên-yeh Ching* in Chinese, translated by Fo-nien towards the end of the third century) that those Bodhisattvas who have not yet entered on the eighth stage (there are ten stages) of Bodhisattvahood may happen to relapse in his religious course, if not be able to receive instruction in the Dharma from some fully enlightened teachers.

[3] Three of the six *gatis* are the *apâyagati* (evil path) : Hell

only said to encourage those novices who are apt to give themselves up to indulgence and so may fail to enter into the right order [i. e., *samyaktvaniyata*], though they may not really fall down [into the evil path].

Further the Bodhisattva has since his first aspiration disciplined himself in those deeds which are beneficial both to himself and others, and thereby his heart has become free from timidity, inasmuch as he would not shudder even at the thought of falling down to the stage of Çrâvakahood or Prayekabuddhahood, any more than to the evil creation (*apâyagati*).

If he learn that he is able to attain to Buddha-hood only after an assiduous observance of various rules of austerity and mortification during immeasurable asamkheya-kalpas,[1] he will never be frightened nor will he falter. How then could he ever raise such thoughts as cherished by Çrâvakas or Pratyekabuddhas? How then could he fall down to the evil creation (*apâyagati*)? He has a firm faith in the truth that all things (*sarvadharma*) from the beginning are in their nature Nirvâna itself.[2]

(*nâraka*); ghost (*preta*); and animal life (*tiryagyoni*). Sometimes demon (*asura*) is added to make the fourth.

[1] For an explanation see. 87, footnote.

[2] The same monistic idea is expressed also in the following famous phrases: "Âçrâvas (desires or prejudices) are nothing but Bodhi (enlightenment), and birth-and-death (or this world of transformation) is nothing but Nirvâna." Individuation is the product of subjectivity; the universe in reality is one great whole.

This sort of aspiration (*cittotpâda*) is more excellent than the former, because the first asamkheya-kalpa of Bodhisattvas of this class is approaching to an end, because they have attained a thorough knowledge of suchness, because all their acts are performed without any stain of attachment.

As they know that the nature of the Dharma, being free from the trace of covetousness, is the perfection of pure and stainless charity (*dânapâramitâ*), they in conformity to it practise charity (*dânapâramitâ*).

As they know that the nature of the Dharma, being free from the influence of the five sensual passions, and, having nothing to do with immorality, is the perfection of pure and stainless morality (*çîlapâramitâ*), they in conformity to it practise morality (*çîlapâramitâ*).

As they know that the nature of the Dharma, having nothing to do with grievance and being free from malice, is the perfection of pure and stainless patience (*kshântipâramitâ*), they in conformity to it practise patience (*kshântipâramitâ*).

As they know that the nature of the Dharma, being free from physical and mental limitations and having nothing to do with indolence, is the perfection of pure and stainless energy (*vîryapâramitâ*), they in conformity to it practise energy (*vîryapâramitâ*).

As they know that the nature of the Dharma, having nothing to do with disturbance or confusion, is the perfection of pure and stainless tranquilisation (*dhyânapâramitâ*), they in conformity to it practise tranquilisation (*dhyânapâramitâ*).

As they know that the nature of the Dharma, being free from the darkness of ignorance, is the perfection of pure and stainless wisdom (*prajñâpâramitâ*), they in conformity to it practise wisdom (*prajñâpâramitâ*).

What is the object of which the Bodhisattva from the stage of pure-heartedness up to the height of Bodhisattvahood has attained an intellectual intuition? The object is no less than suchness itself. We call it an object on account of the evolving-consciousness (*pravrtti-vijñâna*). But in truth there is no object in perfect intellectual intuition, neither is there a subject in it; because the Bodhisattva by means of his wisdom of non-particularisation intuitively perceives suchness (*bhûtatathatâ*) or Dharma-kâya, which is beyond the range of demonstration and argumentation.

Thus he is able in a moment to go over all the worlds in the ten quarters and to make offerings to all Buddhas and to beseech them to revolve the Wheel of the Dharma (*darmacakrapravartana*). His sole desire being to benefit all beings, he does not care for any melodious sounds or words [which he can enjoy in his heavenly abode].[1] In order to encourage weak-hearted people, he shows great energy and

---

[1] In the older translation we read: "Having in view only the emancipation and beneficence of all beings, he [Bodhisattva] does not rely on words and characters."

attains to perfect enlightenment (*anuttarasamyaksam-bodhi*), all at once annihilating the lapse of immeasurable asamkheyakalpas.   Or in order to instigate indolent people, he sometimes attains to Buddhahood only after long discipline and mortification through the period of immeasurable asamkheyakalpas.   The reason why he achieves in this wise infinite methods (*upâya*) [of salvation] is that he wishes thereby to benefit all beings.[1]

But in fact the intrinsic nature, the faculties, the aspiration, and the intellectual attainment of all Bodhisattvas are equal [in value] and there is not any scale of gradation in them.   Because they will all equally and assuredly attain to the most perfect enlightenment, only after the elapsing of three asamkheyakalpas.   Yet as there are differences in various states of existence regarding their objects of seeing, hearing, etc., as well as regarding their faculties, their desires, and their character; so there are correspondingly many different forms of religious discipline [destined to] them.

Three different operations of the mind are revealed in this aspiration by means of intellectual intuition: (1) Pure consciousness originating in the mind as it becomes free from particularisation; (2) moral consciousness [lit., *upâya-citta?*] originating in the mind

---

[1] The older translation reads: "It is out of [human] comprehension that he [Bodhisattva] can achieve such innumerable methods [of salvation]."

as it spontaneously performs those deeds which are beneficent to others; (3) unconscious activity (*karma-vijñânacitta*) originating in the mind as it achieves a most hidden mode of activity.

Again the Bodhisattva, having attained to the perfection of bliss and wisdom, which are his two marks of adornment, has in reaching the height of evolution (*akanishtha*) also obtained the most venerable and excellent body in the whole universe. By means of that knowledge which intuitively identifies itself [with enlightenment *a priori*], he has all at once uprooted ignorance; and thus obtaining omniscience (*sarvâkârajñâna*),[1] he spontaneously achieves incomprehensible [or divine] deeds (*acintyakarma*), reveals himself in immeasurable worlds in the ten quarters, and works out the universal emancipation of mankind.

A question arises here. As space is infinite, worlds are infinite. As worlds are infinite, beings are infinite. As beings are infinite, the modes of mentation are also infinitely diversified. And as all these objects and conditions (*vishaya*) have no limits, they can hardly be known or understood [in all their multitudinousness]. If, now, ignorance being destroyed, all modes

---

[1] A distinction is sometimes made between *Sarvâkârajñâna*, *Sarvajñâna* and *Mârgajñâna*: *Sarvâkârajñâna* is the knowledge by which we are enabled to know all forms and manifestations in their fundamental oneness; *Sarvajñâna* is simply the knowledge of all things, or omniscience; *Mârgajñâna* is the knowledge by which we can recognise the path leading to final emancipation. But they are practically the same.

of mentation are entirely annihilated as well, how can the Bodhisattva understand all things and complete his omniscience (*sarvâkârajñâna*)?

In reply we say: All so-called illusory phenomena are in truth from the beginning what they are; and their essence is nothing but the one soul [or mind]. Though ignorant minds that cling to illusory objects cannot understand that all things are in their nature the highest reality (*paramârtha*), all Buddha-Tathâgatas being free from clinging [or particularising] are able to have an insight into the true nature of things. And by virtue of their great wisdom they illuminate all distinctions between the defiled and the pure; through their immeasurable and inexhaustible sources of expediency (*upâyakauçalya*), which is good and excellent, they benefit and gladden all beings according to the latters' various necessities and capabilities. Therefore the mind that is saturated with subjectivity is annihilated, while all things are understood and omniscience (*sarvâkârajñâna*) is attained.[1]

[1] The older translation reads: "In reply we say: All phenomenal objecs (*vishaya*) are from the beginning [or in their metaphysical origin] of the one mind which is free from imagination and subjectivity. As all beings illusively perceive the existence of the phenomenal world (*vishaya*), they impose limitations on the mind. As they thus illusively cherish imagination and subjectivity, which are not in accordance with the nature of the Dharma, they cannot thoroughly understand it. All Buddha-Tathâgatas are, however, free from illusive perception, and [therefore their knowledge is] omniscient, because the mind constituting the principle of all things is true and valid. The self-essence [of all Buddhas] illuminates all illusive phenomena, possesses a great wisdom-activity and in-

Another question presents itself here : If all Buddhas who are in possession of infinite expediencies (*upâya*) can spontaneously benefit all beings in the ten quarters, why is it that the latter cannot always see Buddhas in person, or witness their divine transformations, or hear their instructions in the Doctrine?

The reply is : Tathâgatas are really in possession of those expediencies, and they are only waiting to reveal themselves to all beings as soon as the latter can purify their own minds.[1]

When a mirror is covered with dust, it cannot reflect images. It can do so only when it is free from stain. It is even the same with all beings. If their minds are not clear of stain, the Dharmakâya cannot reveal itself in them. But if they be freed from stain, then it will reveal itself.

IV. PRACTICE OF FAITH.

In what does the practice of faith (*çraddhâ*) consist?

This part of the Discourse is intended for those beings who have not yet entered into the order of constant truth (*samyaktvaniyata-râçi*).

numerable means [of salvation], whereby, according to the intellectual capacity of all beings, they can reveal to them various significances of the Doctrine. Therefore it is called the *Sarvâkârajnâna.*"

[1] In the older translation we read : " The Dharmakâya of all Buddha-Tathâgatas is universal (*samatâ*) and pervades every thing; it is free from compulsion and therefore spontaneous, manifesting itself through the minds of all beings."

What is meant by faith?   How should one practise faith?

There are four aspects of faith.   [As to faith in
general]: (1) To believe in the fundamental [truth],
that is, to think joyfully of suchness (*bhûtatathatâ*).
[As to particular faiths :] (2) To believe in the Buddha as sufficingly enveloping infinite merits, that is,
to rejoice in worshipping him, in paying homage to
him, in making offerings to him, in hearing the good
doctrine (*saddharma*), in disciplining oneself according
to the doctrine, and in aspiring after omniscience
(*sarvajñâna*). (3) To believe in the Dharma as having
great benefits, that is, to rejoice always in practising
all pâramitâs.   (4) To believe in the Samgha as observing true morality, that is, to be ready to make
offerings to the congregation of Bodhisattvas, and to
practise truthfully all those deeds which are beneficial
at once to oneself and others.

Faith will be perfected by practising the following
five deeds : (1) charity (*dâna*) ; (2) morality (*çîla*);
(3) patience (*kshânti*); (4) energy (*vîrya*); (5) cessation [or tranquilisation, *çamatha*] and intellectual insight (*vidarçana* or *vipaçyana*).

How should people practise charity (*dâna*)?

(1) If persons come and ask them for something,
they should, as far as their means allow, supply it
ungrudgingly and make them rejoice in it. (2) If they
see people threatened with danger, they should try
every means of rescuing them and impart to them a

feeling of fearlessness (*vaiçâradya*). (3) If they have people who come to them desiring instruction in the Doctrine, they should, so far as they are acquainted with it, and, according to their own discretion, deliver speeches on religious discipline.

And when they are performing those three acts of charity, let them not cherish any desire for fame or advantages, nor covet any worldly rewards. Only thinking of those benefits and blessings that are at once for themselves and others, let them aspire to the most excellent, most perfect knowledge (*anuttarasam-yaksambodhi*).

How should they practise morality (*çîla*)?

Those Bodhisattvas who have families [i. e., lay members of Buddhism] should abstain from killing, stealing, adultery, lying, duplicity, slander, frivolous talk, covetousness, malice, currying favor, and false doctrines.[1]

In the case of Çramanas, they should, in order to vanquish all prejudices (*kleça* or *âçrava*), retire from the boisterousness of worldly life, and, abiding in solitude (*aranya*), should practise those deeds which lead to moderation and contentment as well as those of the Dhûtaguna.[2] Even at the violation of minor

[1] Açvaghosha evidently refers to the ten virtues (*daçakuça-lâni*), for which see p. 114, though this list counts more than ten.

[2] There are twelve dhûtagunas or dhûtagangas to be observed by Bhikshus ; *dhûta* means shaking off, that is, shaking off the dust of evil passions : (1) *Paindapâtika*, the rule to live on whatever food they can get by begging from door to door, that they

rules (*çîla*) they should deeply feel fear, shame, and remorse.   Strictly observing all those precepts given by the Tathâgata, they should not call forth the blame or disgust of the outsider, but they should endeavor to induce all beings to abandon the evil and to practise the good.[1]

How should they practise patience (*kshânti*)?

If they meet with the ills of life they should not

may become free from egotism.   (2) *Traicivarika*, the rule allowing the possession of three clothings: *Samghâti*, dress made of scraps ; *Uttarasamghâti*, outer robe ; *Antaravâsaka*, something like skirt.   (3) *Khalupaçcâdbhaktika*, the prohibition of taking any food or beverage when the proper time is over, lest their attention should be disturbed.   (4) *Naishadhyika*, to be in a sitting attitude while sleeping, that they may not become over-indolent· (5) *Yathâsamstarika*, spreading a night-couch where they happen to be.   (6) *Vrkshamûlika*, sitting under a tree.   (7) *Ekâsanika*, taking one meal in a day, that their mental energy may not be weakened by eating too often.   (8) *Abhyavakâçika*, living in an unsheltered place.   (9) *Aranyaka*, leading a solitary, retired life in the wood.   (10) *Cmâçânaka*, abiding in or by a cemetery, that they may constantly ponder on the transiency and uncleanliness of bodily existence.   (11) *Pâmskûlika*, the wearing of the dress made of rags or remnants, that they may have no attachment to luxury.   (12) *Nâmatika*, wearing cloth made of hair. There is a Sûtra named *Twelve Dhûtagunas* among the Chinese collection of the Tripiṭaka.   The list in that book is a little different from what we have here ; the fifth and twelfth are dropped and instead of them we have the rule of begging in due order, corresponding to *Sapadâna-cârikâ* in the Pâli list, and the rule of prohibiting taking too much food at one time, which overtaxing the stomach will obscure the clearness of mind.

[1] The reference is to the threefold precept (*trividhaçîla*) which is (1) the precept of good behavior (*sambhâraçîla*) ; (2) the precept of accumulating virtues (*kuçalasamgrâhaçîla*) ; (3) the precept of being benevolent towards all beings (*sattvârthakriyâçîla*).

shun them. If they suffer sufferings, they should not
feel afflicted. But they should always rejoice in contemplating the deepest significance of the Dharma.[1]

How should they practise energy (*vîrya*)?

Practising all good deeds, they should never indulge in indolence (*kausîdya*). They should think of
all their great mental and physical sufferings, which
they are now vainly suffering on account of their having coveted worldly objects during their existences in
innumerable former ages (*kalpa*), and which do not
give the least nourishment to their spiritual life.
They should, therefore, in order to be emancipated
from those sufferings in the future, be indefatigably
energetic, and never raise the thought of indolence,
but endeavor, out of deep compassion (*mahâkaruna*),
to benefit all beings. Though disciplining themselves
in faith, all novice Bodhisattvas, on account of the
hindrances of their evil karma (*karmâvarana*) produced
by the violation of many important precepts in their
previous existences, may sometimes be annoyed by
evil Mâras, sometimes entangled in worldly engagements, sometimes threatened by various diseases. As
these things will severally disturb their religious course
and make them neglect practising good deeds, they
should dauntlessly, energetically, unintermittently, all

[1] The older translation reads: "Patiently bearing evils in-
flicted by others, they should not cherish any idea of revenge.
They should also bear such [worldly vicissitudes] as prosperity
and decline, reprehension and commendation, renown and defama-
tion, worry and ease, etc."

six watches, day and night, pay homage to all Buddhas, make offerings (*pûjâ*) to them, praise them, re-
pent and confess (*kshamâ*) to them, aspire to the most
excellent knowledge (*samyaksambodhi*), make great
vows (*mahâpranidhâna*); and thereby annihilate the
hindrances of evils and increase the root of merit
(*kuçalamûla*).

How should they practise cessation [or tranquilisation, *çamatha*] and intellectual insight (*vidarçana*
or *vipaçyana*)?

To bring all mental states that produce frivolous
sophistries to a stand is called cessation. To understand adequately the law of causality and transformation is called intellectual insight. Each of them should
be practised separately by the beginner. But when
by degrees he obtains facility and finally attains to
perfection, the two will naturally become harmonised.[1]

Those who practise cessation should dwell in solitude (*âranyaka*) and, sitting cross-legged,[2] rectify the

[1] Observe that cessation should be practised by the beginner,
and for a time only, for the purpose of affording the mind an appreciation of suchness in its purity; the conception of this state of
abstraction should then be harmonised with intellectual insight.
Observe also that the methods of Indian recluses, such as fixing the
breath and going into trances by fixing the thoughts on objects, are
rejected as improper. The practice should assist a beginner to
understand that suchness, though all particulars are dependent on
it, is in its purity a reality.

[2] Those who practise this have to place the left leg above the
right with both close to the body, so that the toes of the left foot
shall rest on the right thigh, and those of the right foot on the left
thigh, while the soles are turned upwards. This posture is con-

attitude and pacify the mind.[1] Do not fix the thoughts on the breath (*ânâpânasmrti*)[2]; do not fix the thoughts on the forms (*samjña*)[3] and colors; do not fix the

sidered to be the best adapted for meditation or for obtaining mental equilibrium.

[1] Among the followers of the Dhyâna sect both in Japan and China, it is customary, while sitting cross-legged and meditating on religious subjects, to expand the abdomen outwards and to breathe very slowly, by which they can, in their opinion, most effectively concentrate their attention and gain perfect mental equilibrium. Prof. J. M. Baldwin in his *Mental Development* says in connexion with bashfulness and modesty, p. 205 footnote : "The only way that I, for one, can undo this distressing outgo of energy, and relieve these uncomfortable inhibitions, is to expand the abdomen by a strong muscular effort and at the same time breathe in as deeply as I can. . . . The comparative relief found in expanding the abdominal muscles is probably due to the fact that it allows the contents of the body to fall, and so relieves the heart from any artificial pressure which may be upon it from the surrounding organs. Further the increased heart-action which is itself a part of shyness requires all the space it can get."

[2] One of the eight subjects of recollection (*anusmrti*), or of the five methods of mental pacification. The eight subjects are : (1) Buddha ; (2) dharma ; (3) samgha ; (4) *çîla*, morality ; (5) *câga* or *tyâga*, liberality ; (6) *deva*, gods ; (7) *ânâpâna*, regulation of inspiration and respiration ; (8) *marana*, death. The five methods are : (1) *Açubhabhâvanâ*, contemplation on the impurity of the body ; (2) *maitrîkarunâ*, love and compassion ; (3) *ânâpânasmrti*, the regulation of inspiration and respiration ; (4) *nidâna*, law of transformation ; (5) *buddhasmrti*, recollection on Buddha.

[3] There are nine Açbhasamjnâs, notions arising from the contemplation of the impurity of a dead body, which is intended to convince one of the fact that our body is not worth while clinging to : (1) Swelling (*vyâdhmataka*) ; (2) fissuring from decay (*vipûyaka*) ; (3) bloody (*vilohita*) ; (4) festering (*vipadumaka*) ; (5) blackish (*vinîlaka*) ; (6) being devoured by animals (*vikhâditaka*) ; (7) scattering (*vikshiptaka*) ; (8) bone (*asthi*) ; (9) burned up (*vidagdhaka*). The Pâli Açubhas count one more.

thoughts on space (*âkâça*) ;[1] do not fix the thoughts
on earth, water, fire, and ether;[1] do not fix the
thoughts on what you see, hear, learn, or memorise
(*vijñânakrtsnâyatana*)[1]. All particularisations, imaginations and recollections should be excluded from
consciousness, even the idea of exclusion being excluded; because [the suchness of] all things is uncreate, eternal, and devoid of all attributes (*alak-
shana*).

[Now in the constant flux of thoughts,] that which
precedes [i. e., a sensation] has been awakened by an
external object ; so the next [step to be taken by the
practiser] is to abandon the idea of an external world.
Then that which succeeds [in that constant flux of
thoughts] is elaborated in his own mind; so he should
in turn abandon reflexion [or thought].   In short, as
his attention is distracted by the external world [outer
vishaya], he is warned to turn it to inner consciousness
[inner *citta*]; while as his retrospection in turn calls
forth a succession of thoughts [or ideal associations],
he is again warned not to attach himself to the latter ;
because, independent of suchness, they [thoughts]
have no existence of their own.

At all times, while moving, standing, sitting, or

---

[1] These constitute the ten *Krtsâyatanas* which are : (1) Blue
(*nîla*); (2) yellow (*pîta*); (3) red (*lohita*); (4) white (*avadâta*);
(5) earth (*prtivî*) ; (6) water (*ap*) ; (7) fire (*tejas*); (8) air (*vâyu*) ;
(9) space (*âkâsa*) ; (10) consciousness (*vijnâna*). The term *Krtsâ-
yâtana* means an universal object or element on which the attention of a samâdhi-practiser is to be fixed.

lying, the practiser should constantly discipline himself as above stated. Gradually entering the samâdhi of suchness,[1] he will finally vanquish all prejudices (*kleça* or *âçrava*), be strengthened in faith (*çraddhâ*), and immediately attain to the state of never-returning (*avaivartikatva*). But those who are sceptical, sacrilegious, destitute of faith, encumbered with the hindrances (*âvarana*) of karma, arrogant, or indolent, are not entitled to enter therein.

And again when the practiser by virtue of his samâdhi[2] attains an immediate insight into the nature of the universe (*dharmadhâtu*), he will recognise that the Dharmakâya of all Tathâgatas and the body of all beings are one and the same (*samatâ*), are consubstantial (*ekalakshana*). On that account it is also called the samâdhi of oneness (*ekalakshanasamâdhi*). By disciplining oneself in this samâdhi, one can obtain in-

---

[1] That is, perfect identification of oneself with suchness.

[2] *Samâdhi* is commonly rendered by ecstasy, trance, concentration, or meditation, all of which are misleading. The term means mental equilibrium, and the reasons why Buddhism recommends the practising of it are, that it helps us in keeping our minds free from disturbance, that it prepares us for a right comprehension of the nature of things, that it subjugates momentary impulses, giving us time for deliberation. Ecstasy or trance, instead of producing those benefits, will lead us to a series of hallucinations, and this is the very opposite of mental quietude. Rhys Davids thinks samâdhi corresponds to faith in Christianity (*S. B. E.*, XI., p. 145), and S. Beal agrees with him in his translation of Açvaghosha's *Buddhacarita*; but I doubt its correctness for the above-stated reasons.

finite samâdhis, because suchness is the source of all samâdhis.

Some people scantily supplied with the root of merit (*kuçalamûla*) may yield to the temptation of Mâras, tîrthakas, or evil spirits. [For instance] those evil ones sometimes assuming horrible forms may frighten the practiser; sometimes manifesting themselves in beautiful figures, they may fascinate him;[1] sometimes appearing in form of a deva, or of a Boddhisattva, or even of a Buddha with all his excellent and magnified features,[2] they may speak about dhârani[3] or the pâramitâ, or may give instructions about various means of emancipation (*mukti*), declaring that there is no hatred, no friendship, no causation, no

---

[1] The older translation has the following passage inserted here: "If he [the practiser] remembers that these are merely subjective, the phenomena will disappear by themselves and will no more trouble him."

[2] Buddha is supposed to have thirty-two general and eighty minor marks of bodily perfection. For particulars see the *Dharmasamgraha*, pp. 18, 19, 51 et seq., edited by Kasawara Kenjiu.

[3] *Dhârani*, which comes from the root *dhr*, meaning to hold, to maintain, to retain, to support, etc., is the name given to any concise statement describing Buddha's virtue, or stating some essential points of Buddhist teachings, or expressing supplication, or containing the exclamations of a vehement feeling; and it implies many significances in a few words, it is a kind of epigram. But later Buddhists came to use the term in quite a different sense; they called a dhârani any tantric expression which was considered to have some mysterious, supernatural powers to bring wealth to destroy enemies, to keep away calamities, etc., etc. Here *dhârani* means simply any epigrammatic proposition which will serve as a key to the deep significance of the Doctrine.

retribution, or declaring that all things in the world are absolute nothingness (*atyantaçûnyatâ*), that they are in their essence Nirvâna itself. Or they may reveal to the practiser his own past and future states of existence, they may teach him to read the thoughts of others,[1] may grant him incomparable power of eloquence, may induce him to crave covetously for worldly fame and advantages.

Further, through the influence of those evil ones the practiser may sometimes be inordinately susceptible to dissatisfaction or delight; he may sometimes be too misanthropic or too philanthropic; he may sometimes be inclined to enjoy drowsiness; he may sometimes not sleep for a long time; he may sometimes be affected by diseases; he may sometimes remain discouraged and indolent; he may sometimes rise all on a sudden with full energy, but only to sink down again into languor; he may sometimes, being over-sceptical, not believe in anything; he may sometimes, abandoning the excellent religious observance, enjoy himself in frivolous occupations, indulge in worldly affairs, gratify his desires and inclinations;

---

[1] Some of these miraculous powers here mentioned are considered to be possessed by the Arhat. Six supernatural faculties (*abhijñâ*) are commonly enumerated: (1) divine eyes (*divyacakshu*) by which the Arhat perceives all that is occurring in the world; (2) the divine hearing (*divyaçrotra*), by which he hears all sounds in the world; (3) reading the thoughts of others (*paracittajñâna*); (4) memory of his former lives (*pûrvanivâsânu-smrti*); (5) miraculous powers (*rddhi*); (6) knowledge how to destroy evil passions (*âçravakshaya*).

he may sometimes attain to the samâdhi of heretics
[i. e., tîrthaka] and, remaining in a state of trance a
day or two, or even seven, and being supplied imagin-
arily with some palatable food and drink, and feeling
very comfortable mentally and physically, he may have
no sensation of hunger or thirst;[1] he may sometimes
be induced to enjoy female fascinations; he may
sometimes be very irregular in taking meals, either
too much or too little; he may sometimes look either
very handsome or very ugly in appearance.

If the practiser get enraptured by those visions
and prejudices (*kleça*), he will lose his root of merit
(*kuçalamûla*) accumulated in his previous existences.
Therefore he should exercise a deep and thorough
contemplation, thinking that all those [heretical states
of samâdhi] are the temptations of Mâras or evil spirits that take advantage of his deficiency in merits and
his intensity of karma-hindrances (*karmâvarana*).

After this thought he should make another thought,
viz., that all these are nothing but mental hallucinations. When he makes these thoughts, the visions
and imaginations will instantly disappear, and, becoming free from all attributes [of limitation], he
will enter into the true samâdhi. He has then not
only liberated himself from all modes of subjectivity,
he has also effaced the idea of suchness. Even when

---

[1] This apparently alludes to the Yoga-praxis, by which man is
said to be able to perform several sorts of miracles beside those
mentioned here.

he rises up from a deep meditation, no visionary images, no prejudices will take possession of in his mind, since he has destroyed the root of illusion through the power of the samâdhi. On the contrary, all the excellent and virtuous deeds which are in conformity with suchness will be constantly performed by him, while all hindrances without exception will be removed by him, who now exhibiting great spiritual energy will never become exhausted.[1]

Those who do not practise this kind of samâdhi will not be able to enter into the essence of the Tathâgata, for all other samâdhis practised in common with the tîrthakas have invariably some attributes [of imperfection] and do not enable one to come into the presence of Buddhas and Bodhisattvas. Therefore let Bodhisattvas [who aspire to the highest knowledge] assiduously apply themselves to the discipline and attain to the perfection of this samâdhi.

[1] The two preceding paragraphs read in the older translation as follows : "On this account, the practiser, always exercising intellectual insight, should save his mind from being entangled in the netting of falsity; he should, dwelling in right contemplation, not cling or attach [to any object], and thereby he will be able to liberate himself from all kinds of karma-hindrance. It should be known that all samâdhis practised by heretics [i. e., tîrthaka] are invariably the production of the [egoistic] conception and desire and self-assumption, that they are hankering after worldly renown advantages, and reverence. The samâdhi of suchness [on the other hand] has nothing to do with subjectivity and attachment. If one is free from indolence even when rising from meditation one's prejudices will by degrees get attenuated."

Those who practise this samâdhi will procure in their present life ten beneficial results:

1. They will always be remembered and guarded by all Buddhas and Bodhisattvas in all quarters.

2. They will not be molested by Mâras or evil spirits.

3. They will not be led astray by false doctrines.[1]

4. They will be free from disparaging the deepest Doctrine (*gambhîradharma*). Their serious misdemeanors as well as their karma-hindrances will be attenuated.

5. They will destroy all doubts, sinful recollections, and contemplations.

6. They will be strengthened in their belief in the spiritual state of Tathâgata.

7. They will be liberated from gloomy remorse; they will be courageous and unflinching in the face of birth and death.

8. Being free from arrogance and presumptuousness, they will be meek and patient and will be revered by all the world.

9. If not practising deep meditation, those prejudices (*âçrava*) which are now getting weaker, will not assert themselves in them.

10. While practising meditation, they will not be disturbed by any external objects, such as voices, sounds, etc.

---

[1] The older translation reads: "the ninety-five heretical doctrines."

But mind : when the practiser is trained only in cessation (çamatha), his mind will sink down into stupidity, and acquiring a habit of indolence, cannot rejoice in doing good acts, as he will estrange himself from deep compassion (mahâkaruna). Accordingly he should discipline himself in intellectual insight (vidarçana) as well.

In what does this discipline consist?

The practiser should contemplate that all things in the world are subject to a constant transformation, that since they are transient they are misery, that since they are misery they are not things-in-themselves [i. e., âtman].[1]

He should contemplate that all things in the past are like a dream, those in the present are like the lightning, those in the future are like clouds that spontaneously come into existence.

He should contemplate that all that has a body is impure, being a lodging place of obnoxious vermin and the intermixture of prejudices (âçrava).

Contemplate that ignorant minds, on account of their groundless imagination, take the unreal as they see it, for reality.

Contemplate that all objects which come into existence by a combination of various causes (prat-

---

[1] The idea is: that which is transient is dependent, conditional and not self-regulating ; and that which is without freedom is necessarily miserable, that is to say, it has no self-regulating âtman within itself.

yaya) are like a chimera, having [only a transitory existence and] no [genuine] realness at all.

Contemplate that the highest truth (*paramârtha-satya*) is not a production of mind [or subjectivity], cannot be [fully] illustrated by analogy, cannot be [exhaustively] treated by reasoning.[1]

Contemplate that on account of the perfuming power of ignorance (*avidya*) all beings from eternity suffer great mental and physical sufferings in immeasurable ways; that those immeasurable and innumerable sufferings are suffered in the present and will be suffered in the future; that while it is extremely difficult to disentangle, to emancipate themselves from those sufferings, all beings always abiding in the midst of them are not conscious of the fact, and this makes them the more pitiable.

After these contemplations the practiser should awake positive knowledge [or unerring understanding], feel the highest and deepest compassion (*karuna*) for all suffering beings, rouse dauntless energy, and make great vows (*mahâpranidhâna*) as follows:

" May my mind be freed from all contradictions; may I abandon particularisation; may I personally attend on all Buddhas and Bodhisattvas, whom I shall pay homage to, make offerings to, revere and praise, and to whose instructions in the good Doctrine (*saddharma*) I shall listen; may I truthfully discipline myself according to their teachings, and to the end of

[1] The last three clauses are missing in the older translation.

the future never be negligent in self-discipline; may I
with innumerable expediencies (*upâya*) [of salvation]
deliver all beings who are drowned in the sea of misery, and bring them to the highest bliss of Nirvâna."

After these vows the practiser should at all times,
so far as his energy permits, practise those deeds
which are beneficial both to himself and others. While
moving, standing, sitting, or lying, he should assiduously meditate what should be done and what should
be avoided. This is called the practising of intellectual
insight (*vidarçana* or *vipaçyana*).

And again when the practiser disciplines himself
only in intellectual insight his mind may lack tranquilisation, and becoming too susceptible to scepti-
cism, may not be in accord with the highest truth,
may not attain to the wisdom of non-particularisation.
Therefore cessation and intellectual insight should be
practised side by side. He should consider that nothing is self-existent (*svabhâva*), and things [in their
essence] are uncreate, eternally tranquil, and Nirvâna
itself. But at the same time let him not forget to reflect that karma and its retribution, both good and
evil, being produced by a co-operation of principle
and conditions, will neither be lost nor destroyed.
He should thus ponder on the law of causation, both
in its good and evil karma and retribution, but at the
same time let him not forget to perceive that all
things, though in their essence uncreate, have no self-
existence, etc., they are Nirvâna.

By practising cessation, common people (*prthag-jana*) will be cured of finding pleasures in worldli-ness, while Çrâvakas and Pratyekabuddhas will be cured of feeling intimidation at the thought of birth and death.

By practising intellectual insight common people will be cured of not cultivating their root of merit (*kuçalamûla*), while Çrâvakas and Pratyekabuddhas will be cured of narrow-mindedness whereby they can-not raise deep compassion [for mankind].

Therefore, cessation and intellectual insight are supplementary to, not independent of, each other. If one of the two is wanting, the practiser will surely be unable to attain to the most excellant knowledge (*bodhiparinishpatti*).

And again when those novice Bodhisattvas who are living in this present life [*sahâlokadhâtu*, i. e., the enduring world of actual existence], may sometimes suffer misfortunes that are caused by climate, weather, unforeseen famine, or what not; and when they wit-ness those people who are immoral, fearful, infatuated with the three venomous passions (*akuçalamûla*), cling to false and self-contradictory doctrines, desert the good law and acquire evil habits; they [that is, novice Bodhisattvas], living in the midst of them, may feel so discouraged that they may come to doubt whether they can see Buddhas and Bodhisattvas, whether they can actualise their pure and spotless faith (*çraddhâ*).

Therefore, it is advisable for those novices to cher-

ish this thought: All Buddhas and Bodhisattvas in
the ten quarters having great, unimpeded supernatural powers (*abhijñâ*), are able to emancipate all suffering beings by means of various expediencies that
are good and excellent (*upâyakauçalya*).

After this reflexion, they should make great vows
(*mahâpranidhâna*), and with full concentration of spiritual powers think of Buddhas and Bodhisattvas
When they have such a firm conviction, free from all
doubts, they will assuredly be able to be born in the
Buddha-country beyond (*buddha-kshetra*), when they
pass away from this present life, and seeing there
Buddhas and Bodhisattvas, to complete their faith and
to eternally escape from all evil creations (*apâya*).[1]

Therefore, it is said in the Sûtra[2] that if devoted

[1] The same idea of salvation is expressed in the *Bhagavadgîtâ*, Chap. VIII., p. 78 : "And he who leaves this body and de-
parts (from this world) remembering me in (his) last moment,
comes into my essence.   There is no doubt of that. . . . Therefore
at all times remember me. . . . Fixing your mind and understanding on me you will come to me, there is no doubt   He who thinks
of the supreme divine being, O son of Prithâ ! with the mind not
(running) to other (objects), and possessed of abstraction in the
shape of continuous meditation (about the Supreme) goes to him.'

[2] It is not exactly known from what Sûtra this passage is taken,
but it is not difficult to discover similar passages in the Sûtras
which constitute the canonical books of the Sukhâvatî sect, i. e.,
in the larger or smaller *Sukhâvatî-vyûha*, or in the *Amitâyur-
dhyâna*.   I here quote such a passage from Max Müller's English
translation of the larger *Sukhâvatî-vyûha-Sûtra*, Sec. XXVII.:
"And if, O Ânanda, any son or daughter of a good family should
wish—What ?—How then may I see that Tathâgata Amitâbha vis-
ibly, then he must raise his thought on to the highest perfect knowl
edge, he must direct his thought with perseverance and excessive

men and women would be filled with concentration of
thought, think of Amitâbha Buddha in the world of
highest happiness (*sukhâvatî*) in the Western region,
and direct (*parinâma*) all the root of their good work
toward being born there, they would assuredly be born
there.

Thus always seeing Buddhas there, their faith will
be strengthened, and they will never relapse therefrom.
Receiving instruction in the doctrine, and recognising
the Dharmakâya of the Buddha, they will by gradual
discipline be able to enter upon the state of truth
[i. e., Buddhahood] (*samyaktva-râçi*).

V. BENEFITS.

In what does this part [treating] of the benefits
consist?

Such as above presented is the spiritual significance of the Mahâyâna, and I have finished elucidating it.

Those who, desiring to produce pure and spotless
faith in, and knowledge of, the deepest spiritual con-

desire towards that Buddha country, and direct the stock of his
good works towards being born there." As I noticed elsewhere, if
those Mahâyâna texts had been considered at the time of Açvaghosha, that is, in the first century after or before Christ, as a genuine teaching of Buddha, then it would have to be admitted, it
seems to me, that the Mahâyâna system existed at an early stage
of the development of Buddhism, most probably side by side with
Hînayânism, which is generally supposed by Pâli scholars to be
more primitive. But the history of Buddhism in India as a whole
is still veiled with dark clouds of uncertainty, in spite of the fact
that quite a few original Sanskrit texts have been recovered.

dition and the greatest Dharma of the Tathâgata, so
that they have no hindrances in entering upon the
Mahâyâna path (*mârga*), will diligently pursue this
brief discourse, contemplate it, discipline themselves
in it, and thus 'they can surely and unhesitatingly attain to the knowledge of all forms and manifestations
(*sarvâkârajñâna*).

And if they do not awake a feeling of fear in hearing this Doctrine, they will surely be qualified to inherit the Buddha-seeds and immediately receive the
prophecy (*vijâkarana*)[1] from the Buddha. Even if
there be a person who could convert all beings in three
thousand great chiliocosms (*trisâhasramahâsâhasra*),[2]
and could induce them to observe the ten precepts of
morality (*daçakuçalamârga*), his merits will not be su-

---

[1] This is not a mere prophecy of one's destiny, but Buddha's
assurance for those Bodhisattvas who, having accumulated sufficient amount of merits, are qualified to attain in the future the
most excellent, perfect knowledge and to achieve final salvation
both for themselves and for all other beings. See how five hundred disciples received this assurance from Buddha in the *Sad-
dharmapundarîka Sûtra*, Chap. VIII.

[2] Our earth which was supposed by ancient Indians to be flat,
infinitely extending in space, is not the only region inhabited by
sentient beings; but there are innumerable worlds outside of this
Manushyalokadhâtu, which exist above as well as below us. Now
according to the *Abhidharmakoça-çâstra* by Vasubandhu, a small
chiliocosm (*sâhasralokadhâtu*) consists of one thousand of Rûpa-
lokas and of the first Dhyâna heavens, and one thousand of small
chiliocosms make a middling chiliocosm, a thousand of which in
turn making a great chiliocosm. So we may take the great chiliocosm (*mahâsâhasralokadhâtu*) as including all possible heavenly
bodies which fill up this boundless space.

perior to those of the person who will truthfully comprehend this Doctrine even for a second; because the merits of the latter immeasurably and infinitely surpass those of the former.

If one practise this doctrine as it is instructed for one whole day and night, the merits thereby produced will be so immeasurable, infinite, inconceivable that all Buddhas in the ten quarters could not exhaust them, even if each of them continued to praise them for innumerable asamkheyakalpas.[1] As the merits of suchness have no limits, so the merits of the discipline are also without limit.

Those who slander this doctrine, on the other hand, commit immeasurable faults and suffer great sufferings for asamkheyakalpas. Accordingly all beings should cherish a firm faith in the Doctrine and never slander it, for this will lead to the destruction of oneself as well as others, nay, even to the destruction of the seeds of the Triple Treasure (*triratna*).

By practising this Doctrine all Buddhas have attained the most excellent knowledge (*anuttarajñânâ*). By practising this Doctrine all Bodhisattvas have obtained an insight into the Dhamrakâya of the Tathâgata.

By practising this Doctrine Bodhisattvas in the past consummated, Bodhisattvas in the future will consummate, pure and spotless faith (*çraddhâ*) in the Mahâyâna. Therefore those who desire to practise

[1] For an explanation see the footnote to *kalpa*, p. 87.

those excellent virtues that are beneficial at once to themselves and others should diligently study this Discourse.

I have now finished elucidating
The deepest and greatest significance [of the
    Dharma].
May its merit be distributed among all creatures,
And make them understand the Doctrine of Such-
    ness.

GLOSSARY.

Activity-consciousness 業識 *yeh shih, karmavijnâna?* the assertion of the "Will to Live."

Affectional hindrance 煩惱障 *fan nao chang, kleçâvarana,* hindrance to the attainment of Nirvâna, arising from the assertion of the "Will to Live."

Affirmation, or Non-emptiness, 不空 *pu k'ung, açûnyatâ,* suchness as constituting the basis of reality ; it is equivalent to the Tathâgata's Womb.

All-conserving mind, The, 阿賴耶識 *a lai ya shih,* or *tsang shih,* or 阿梨耶 *a li ya,* 無沒識 *mu mo shih, âlaya-vijnâna,* a stage in the evolution of suchness, in which consciousness is awakened to recognise a distinction between suchness and birth-and-death.

Aspiration 發心 *fa hsin, cittotpâda,* desire to attain the most perfect knowledge.

Âtman 我 *wu,* (1) ego-soul ; (2) noumenon or thing-in-itself. Anâtman is a negative form of the same.

Birth-and-death 生滅 *shêng mieh, samsâra,* the material principle in contradistinction to the formal principle, suchness.

Consciousness 識 *shih, vijnâna,* mentation in general.

Defilement 染 *jan,* a cognisance of dual aspect of suchness ; not necessarily moral or intellectual fault.

Dharma 法 *fa,* (1) that which subsists, or substance ; (2) law, doctrine, or regulative principle.

Dharmakâya 法身 *fa shên,* absolute being, or absolute knowledge when considered from the idealistic point of view.

Ego 意 *i, manas,* the subjective mind which believes consciously or unconsciously in the existence of the ego-soul.

Ego-consciousness 意識 *i shih, manovijnâna*, egocentric thoughts in general ; the mind that makes a deliberate assumption of a dualistic existence of the ego and the non-ego.

Enlightenment 覺 *chiao (buddhi?)*, another name for suchness, psychologically considered.

Evolving-consciousness 轉識 *chuan shih, pravrtti-vijnâna*, a state of suchness out of which mentation in general evolves.

Ignorance 無明 *wu ming, avidya*, a state of suchness in its evolution ; practically the same as birth-and-death.

Intellectual hindrance 所知障 *so chih chang, jneyâvarana*, the hindrance to the attainment of Nirvâna, which arises from intellectual prejudices.

Interrelated defilement 相應染 *hsiang ying jan*, a conscious assertion of dualism.

Karma-hindrance, *yeh chang, karmâvarana*, the hindrance in the way to Nirvâna, that is brought forth by evil deeds done in previous lives.

Mahâyâna 大乘 *tai chang*, literally, great conveyance, another name for suchness.

Means, or expediency 方便 *fang pien, upâya*, when philosophically considered, the process of evolution, whereby the unconditional suchness becomes conditional.

Mind 心 *hsin, citta*, relative aspect of suchness. Soul, mind, and suchness are to a certain extent synonymous, but in this translation the following distinction is made : Suchness, when unqualified, signifies its absolute aspect and is practically the same with the soul, while the term mind is used to denote a state of suchness in its operation or evolution.

Negation, or emptiness 空 *k'ung, çûnyatâ*, an aspect of suchness as transcending all forms of relativitity.

Nirvâna 涅槃 *nieh p'an*, the recognition of the truth or suchness.

Non-enlightenment 不覺 *pu chiao (nirbuddhi?)*, another name for ignorance, psychologically considered. Non-enlightenment, defilement, birth-and-death, and ignorance, are more or less synonymous and interchangeable.

Non-particularisation 無分別 *wu fên pieh*, the subjective attitude that is free from a deliberate assertion of dualism ; i is similar in a sense to Lao-Tze's "Non-assertion."

Not-interrelated defilement 不相應染 *pu hsiang ying jan*, an unconscious assertion of dualism.

Particularisation-consciousness 分別識 *fên pieh shih*, the consciousness that adheres to the dual aspect of existence; a synonym of phenomena-particularising-consciousness.

Prejudice 煩惱 *fan nao*, *âçrava* or *kleça*, the subjectivity that averts the due exercise of will and intellect.

Samâdhi 三昧 *san mei*, or 定 *ting*, literally equilibrium, a state of consciousness in which all modes of mental activity are in equilibrium.

Soul 心 *hsin*, *hrdaya* or *citta*, that which constitutes the kernel of things, but not in the Christian conception of the word; a synonym of absolute suchness.

Soul as birth-and-death, 心生滅 *hsin shêng mieh*, relative aspect of suchness as material principle; a synonym of ignorance.

Soul as suchness 心眞如 *hsin chen ju*, absolute aspect of suchness as purely formal.

Subjectivity 妄念 *wang nien*, or 妄念心 *wang nien hsin*, or 心念 *hsin nien*, or simply 念 *nien*, *smrti*, literally, recollection or memory, or 分別 *fên piéh*, particularisation; the mentation that is not in accordance with the conception of suchness.

Suchness 眞如 *chên ju*, *bhûtatathatâ*, the highest reality, or the "purely formal" aspect of existence.

Tathâgata's womb 如來藏 *ju lai tsang*, *tathâgata-garbha*, a state of suchness as containing every possible merit.

Totality of things 法界 *fah chieh*, *dharmadhâtu*, literally, the basis of things, that is, the universe as a whole.

Vow 願 *yüan*, or 誓願 *shih yüan*, *pranidhâna*, commonly translated prayer, but not in the Christian sense, for Buddhists think that a vow or vehement desire has power enough to achieve what is desired, according to their idealistic conception of the world.

CORRIGENDA.

Page 3, line 2, read *gâthâ* for *ghâtâs.*
" 5, " 8, " *Fo* for *Fa.*
" 12, " 13, " *peace* for *piece.*
" 12, " 20, " [3] for [1].
" 18, " 22, " *fasciculus* for *fasciculi.*
" 24, " 12, " *conversion* for *conversions.*
" 36, " 4, " *non-âtman* for *none-âtman.*
" 60, " 5, " *çûnyatâ* for *çûnjatâ.*
" 60, " 10, insert *that* after *understanding.*
" 119, " 1, read *Anupadiçesha* for *Anupadhiçesa.*
" 126, " 17, " *latter's* for *latters'.*

INDEX.

A CATALOG OF SELECTED
DOVER BOOKS
IN ALL FIELDS OF INTEREST

A CATALOG OF SELECTED DOVER

BOOKS IN ALL FIELDS OF INTEREST

CONCERNING THE SPIRITUAL IN ART, Wassily Kandinsky. Pioneering work by father of abstract art. Thoughts on color theory, nature of art. Analysis of earlier masters. 12 illustrations. 80pp. of text. 5⅜ x 8½.   23411-8

ANIMALS: 1,419 Copyright-Free Illustrations of Mammals, Birds, Fish, Insects, etc., Jim Harter (ed.). Clear wood engravings present, in extremely lifelike poses, over 1,000 species of animals. One of the most extensive pictorial sourcebooks of its kind. Captions. Index. 284pp. 9 x 12.   23766-4

CELTIC ART: The Methods of Construction, George Bain. Simple geometric techniques for making Celtic interlacements, spirals, Kells-type initials, animals, humans, etc. Over 500 illustrations. 160pp. 9 x 12. (Available in U.S. only.)   22923-8

AN ATLAS OF ANATOMY FOR ARTISTS, Fritz Schider. Most thorough reference work on art anatomy in the world. Hundreds of illustrations, including selections from works by Vesalius, Leonardo, Goya, Ingres, Michelangelo, others. 593 illustrations. 192pp. 7⅛ x 10¼.   20241-0

CELTIC HAND STROKE-BY-STROKE (Irish Half-Uncial from "The Book of Kells"): An Arthur Baker Calligraphy Manual, Arthur Baker. Complete guide to creating each letter of the alphabet in distinctive Celtic manner. Covers hand position, strokes, pens, inks, paper, more. Illustrated. 48pp. 8¼ x 11.   24336-2

EASY ORIGAMI, John Montroll. Charming collection of 32 projects (hat, cup, pelican, piano, swan, many more) specially designed for the novice origami hobbyist. Clearly illustrated easy-to-follow instructions insure that even beginning papercrafters will achieve successful results. 48pp. 8¼ x 11.   27298-2

THE COMPLETE BOOK OF BIRDHOUSE CONSTRUCTION FOR WOODWORKERS, Scott D. Campbell. Detailed instructions, illustrations, tables. Also data on bird habitat and instinct patterns. Bibliography. 3 tables. 63 illustrations in 15 figures. 48pp. 5¼ x 8½.   24407-5

BLOOMINGDALE'S ILLUSTRATED 1886 CATALOG: Fashions, Dry Goods and Housewares, Bloomingdale Brothers. Famed merchants' extremely rare catalog depicting about 1,700 products: clothing, housewares, firearms, dry goods, jewelry, more. Invaluable for dating, identifying vintage items. Also, copyright-free graphics for artists, designers. Co-published with Henry Ford Museum & Greenfield Village. 160pp. 8¼ x 11.   25780-0

HISTORIC COSTUME IN PICTURES, Braun & Schneider. Over 1,450 costumed figures in clearly detailed engravings–from dawn of civilization to end of 19th century. Captions. Many folk costumes. 256pp. 8⅜ x 11¾.   23150-X

STICKLEY CRAFTSMAN FURNITURE CATALOGS, Gustav Stickley and L. & J. G. Stickley. Beautiful, functional furniture in two authentic catalogs from 1910. 594 illustrations, including 277 photos, show settles, rockers, armchairs, reclining chairs, bookcases, desks, tables. 183pp. 6½ x 9¼.   23838-5

AMERICAN LOCOMOTIVES IN HISTORIC PHOTOGRAPHS: 1858 to 1949, Ron Ziel (ed.). A rare collection of 126 meticulously detailed official photographs, called "builder portraits," of American locomotives that majestically chronicle the rise of steam locomotive power in America. Introduction. Detailed captions. xi+ 129pp. 9 x 12.   27393-8

AMERICA'S LIGHTHOUSES: An Illustrated History, Francis Ross Holland, Jr. Delightfully written, profusely illustrated fact-filled survey of over 200 American lighthouses since 1716. History, anecdotes, technological advances, more. 240pp. 8 x 10¾.
25576-X

TOWARDS A NEW ARCHITECTURE, Le Corbusier. Pioneering manifesto by founder of "International School." Technical and aesthetic theories, views of industry, economics, relation of form to function, "mass-production split" and much more. Profusely illustrated. 320pp. 6⅛ x 9¼. (Available in U.S. only.)   25023-7

HOW THE OTHER HALF LIVES, Jacob Riis. Famous journalistic record, exposing poverty and degradation of New York slums around 1900, by major social reformer. 100 striking and influential photographs. 233pp. 10 x 7⅞.   22012-5

FRUIT KEY AND TWIG KEY TO TREES AND SHRUBS, William M. Harlow. One of the handiest and most widely used identification aids. Fruit key covers 120 deciduous and evergreen species; twig key 160 deciduous species. Easily used. Over 300 photographs. 126pp. 5⅜ x 8½.   20511-8

COMMON BIRD SONGS, Dr. Donald J. Borror. Songs of 60 most common U.S. birds: robins, sparrows, cardinals, bluejays, finches, more—arranged in order of increasing complexity. Up to 9 variations of songs of each species.
Cassette and manual 99911-4

ORCHIDS AS HOUSE PLANTS, Rebecca Tyson Northen. Grow cattleyas and many other kinds of orchids—in a window, in a case, or under artificial light. 63 illustrations. 148pp. 5⅜ x 8½.   23261-1

MONSTER MAZES, Dave Phillips. Masterful mazes at four levels of difficulty. Avoid deadly perils and evil creatures to find magical treasures. Solutions for all 32 exciting illustrated puzzles. 48pp. 8¼ x 11.   26005-4

MOZART'S DON GIOVANNI (DOVER OPERA LIBRETTO SERIES), Wolfgang Amadeus Mozart. Introduced and translated by Ellen H. Bleiler. Standard Italian libretto, with complete English translation. Convenient and thoroughly portable—an ideal companion for reading along with a recording or the performance itself. Introduction. List of characters. Plot summary. 121pp. 5¼ x 8½.   24944-1

TECHNICAL MANUAL AND DICTIONARY OF CLASSICAL BALLET, Gail Grant. Defines, explains, comments on steps, movements, poses and concepts. 15-page pictorial section. Basic book for student, viewer. 127pp. 5⅜ x 8½.   21843-0

THE CLARINET AND CLARINET PLAYING, David Pino. Lively, comprehensive work features suggestions about technique, musicianship, and musical interpretation, as well as guidelines for teaching, making your own reeds, and preparing for public performance. Includes an intriguing look at clarinet history. "A godsend," *The Clarinet*, Journal of the International Clarinet Society. Appendixes. 7 illus. 320pp. 5⅜ x 8½. 40270-3

HOLLYWOOD GLAMOR PORTRAITS, John Kobal (ed.). 145 photos from 1926-49. Harlow, Gable, Bogart, Bacall; 94 stars in all. Full background on photographers, technical aspects. 160pp. 8⅜ x 11¼. 23352-9

THE ANNOTATED CASEY AT THE BAT: A Collection of Ballads about the Mighty Casey/Third, Revised Edition, Martin Gardner (ed.). Amusing sequels and parodies of one of America's best-loved poems: Casey's Revenge, Why Casey Whiffed, Casey's Sister at the Bat, others. 256pp. 5⅜ x 8½. 28598-7

THE RAVEN AND OTHER FAVORITE POEMS, Edgar Allan Poe. Over 40 of the author's most memorable poems: "The Bells," "Ulalume," "Israfel," "To Helen," "The Conqueror Worm," "Eldorado," "Annabel Lee," many more. Alphabetic lists of titles and first lines. 64pp. 5$\frac{3}{16}$ x 8¼. 26685-0

PERSONAL MEMOIRS OF U. S. GRANT, Ulysses Simpson Grant. Intelligent, deeply moving firsthand account of Civil War campaigns, considered by many the finest military memoirs ever written. Includes letters, historic photographs, maps and more. 528pp. 6⅛ x 9¼. 28587-1

ANCIENT EGYPTIAN MATERIALS AND INDUSTRIES, A. Lucas and J. Harris. Fascinating, comprehensive, thoroughly documented text describes this ancient civilization's vast resources and the processes that incorporated them in daily life, including the use of animal products, building materials, cosmetics, perfumes and incense, fibers, glazed ware, glass and its manufacture, materials used in the mummification process, and much more. 544pp. 6⅛ x 9¼. (Available in U.S. only.) 40446-3

RUSSIAN STORIES/RUSSKIE RASSKAZY: A Dual-Language Book, edited by Gleb Struve. Twelve tales by such masters as Chekhov, Tolstoy, Dostoevsky, Pushkin, others. Excellent word-for-word English translations on facing pages, plus teaching and study aids, Russian/English vocabulary, biographical/critical introductions, more. 416pp. 5⅜ x 8½. 26244-8

PHILADELPHIA THEN AND NOW: 60 Sites Photographed in the Past and Present, Kenneth Finkel and Susan Oyama. Rare photographs of City Hall, Logan Square, Independence Hall, Betsy Ross House, other landmarks juxtaposed with contemporary views. Captures changing face of historic city. Introduction. Captions. 128pp. 8¼ x 11. 25790-8

AIA ARCHITECTURAL GUIDE TO NASSAU AND SUFFOLK COUNTIES, LONG ISLAND, The American Institute of Architects, Long Island Chapter, and the Society for the Preservation of Long Island Antiquities. Comprehensive, well-researched and generously illustrated volume brings to life over three centuries of Long Island's great architectural heritage. More than 240 photographs with authoritative, extensively detailed captions. 176pp. 8¼ x 11. 26946-9

NORTH AMERICAN INDIAN LIFE: Customs and Traditions of 23 Tribes, Elsie Clews Parsons (ed.). 27 fictionalized essays by noted anthropologists examine religion, customs, government, additional facets of life among the Winnebago, Crow, Zuni, Eskimo, other tribes. 480pp. 6⅛ x 9¼. 27377-6

FRANK LLOYD WRIGHT'S DANA HOUSE, Donald Hoffmann. Pictorial essay of residential masterpiece with over 160 interior and exterior photos, plans, elevations, sketches and studies. 128pp. 9¼ x 10¾. 29120-0

THE MALE AND FEMALE FIGURE IN MOTION: 60 Classic Photographic Sequences, Eadweard Muybridge. 60 true-action photographs of men and women walking, running, climbing, bending, turning, etc., reproduced from rare 19th-century masterpiece. vi + 121pp. 9 x 12. 24745-7

1001 QUESTIONS ANSWERED ABOUT THE SEASHORE, N. J. Berrill and Jacquelyn Berrill. Queries answered about dolphins, sea snails, sponges, starfish, fishes, shore birds, many others. Covers appearance, breeding, growth, feeding, much more. 305pp. 5¼ x 8¼. 23366-9

ATTRACTING BIRDS TO YOUR YARD, William J. Weber. Easy-to-follow guide offers advice on how to attract the greatest diversity of birds: birdhouses, feeders, water and waterers, much more. 96pp. 5³⁄₁₆ x 8¼. 28927-3

MEDICINAL AND OTHER USES OF NORTH AMERICAN PLANTS: A Historical Survey with Special Reference to the Eastern Indian Tribes, Charlotte Erichsen-Brown. Chronological historical citations document 500 years of usage of plants, trees, shrubs native to eastern Canada, northeastern U.S. Also complete identifying information. 343 illustrations. 544pp. 6½ x 9¼. 25951-X

STORYBOOK MAZES, Dave Phillips. 23 stories and mazes on two-page spreads: Wizard of Oz, Treasure Island, Robin Hood, etc. Solutions. 64pp. 8¼ x 11. 23628-5

AMERICAN NEGRO SONGS: 230 Folk Songs and Spirituals, Religious and Secular, John W. Work. This authoritative study traces the African influences of songs sung and played by black Americans at work, in church, and as entertainment. The author discusses the lyric significance of such songs as "Swing Low, Sweet Chariot," "John Henry," and others and offers the words and music for 230 songs. Bibliography. Index of Song Titles. 272pp. 6½ x 9¼. 40271-1

MOVIE-STAR PORTRAITS OF THE FORTIES, John Kobal (ed.). 163 glamor, studio photos of 106 stars of the 1940s: Rita Hayworth, Ava Gardner, Marlon Brando, Clark Gable, many more. 176pp. 8⅜ x 11¼. 23546-7

BENCHLEY LOST AND FOUND, Robert Benchley. Finest humor from early 30s, about pet peeves, child psychologists, post office and others. Mostly unavailable elsewhere. 73 illustrations by Peter Arno and others. 183pp. 5⅜ x 8½. 22410-4

YEKL and THE IMPORTED BRIDEGROOM AND OTHER STORIES OF YIDDISH NEW YORK, Abraham Cahan. Film Hester Street based on *Yekl* (1896). Novel, other stories among first about Jewish immigrants on N.Y.'s East Side. 240pp. 5⅜ x 8½. 22427-9

SELECTED POEMS, Walt Whitman. Generous sampling from *Leaves of Grass*. Twenty-four poems include "I Hear America Singing," "Song of the Open Road," "I Sing the Body Electric," "When Lilacs Last in the Dooryard Bloom'd," "O Captain! My Captain!"–all reprinted from an authoritative edition. Lists of titles and first lines. 128pp. 5³⁄₁₆ x 8¼. 26878-0

THE BEST TALES OF HOFFMANN, E. T. A. Hoffmann. 10 of Hoffmann's most important stories: "Nutcracker and the King of Mice," "The Golden Flowerpot," etc. 458pp. 5⅜ x 8½.   21793-0

FROM FETISH TO GOD IN ANCIENT EGYPT, E. A. Wallis Budge. Rich detailed survey of Egyptian conception of "God" and gods, magic, cult of animals, Osiris, more. Also, superb English translations of hymns and legends. 240 illustrations. 545pp. 5⅜ x 8½.   25803-3

FRENCH STORIES/CONTES FRANÇAIS: A Dual-Language Book, Wallace Fowlie. Ten stories by French masters, Voltaire to Camus: "Micromegas" by Voltaire; "The Atheist's Mass" by Balzac; "Minuet" by de Maupassant; "The Guest" by Camus, six more. Excellent English translations on facing pages. Also French-English vocabulary list, exercises, more. 352pp. 5⅜ x 8½.   26443-2

CHICAGO AT THE TURN OF THE CENTURY IN PHOTOGRAPHS: 122 Historic Views from the Collections of the Chicago Historical Society, Larry A. Viskochil. Rare large-format prints offer detailed views of City Hall, State Street, the Loop, Hull House, Union Station, many other landmarks, circa 1904-1913. Introduction. Captions. Maps. 144pp. 9⅜ x 12¼.   24656-6

OLD BROOKLYN IN EARLY PHOTOGRAPHS, 1865-1929, William Lee Younger. Luna Park, Gravesend race track, construction of Grand Army Plaza, moving of Hotel Brighton, etc. 157 previously unpublished photographs. 165pp. 8⅞ x 11¾.
                                                                                        23587-4

THE MYTHS OF THE NORTH AMERICAN INDIANS, Lewis Spence. Rich anthology of the myths and legends of the Algonquins, Iroquois, Pawnees and Sioux, prefaced by an extensive historical and ethnological commentary. 36 illustrations. 480pp. 5⅜ x 8½.   25967-6

AN ENCYCLOPEDIA OF BATTLES: Accounts of Over 1,560 Battles from 1479 B.C. to the Present, David Eggenberger. Essential details of every major battle in recorded history from the first battle of Megiddo in 1479 B.C. to Grenada in 1984. List of Battle Maps. New Appendix covering the years 1967-1984. Index. 99 illustrations. 544pp. 6½ x 9¼.   24913-1

SAILING ALONE AROUND THE WORLD, Captain Joshua Slocum. First man to sail around the world, alone, in small boat. One of great feats of seamanship told in delightful manner. 67 illustrations. 294pp. 5⅜ x 8½.   20326-3

ANARCHISM AND OTHER ESSAYS, Emma Goldman. Powerful, penetrating, prophetic essays on direct action, role of minorities, prison reform, puritan hypocrisy, violence, etc. 271pp. 5⅜ x 8½.   22484-8

MYTHS OF THE HINDUS AND BUDDHISTS, Ananda K. Coomaraswamy and Sister Nivedita. Great stories of the epics; deeds of Krishna, Shiva, taken from puranas, Vedas, folk tales; etc. 32 illustrations. 400pp. 5⅜ x 8½.   21759-0

THE TRAUMA OF BIRTH, Otto Rank. Rank's controversial thesis that anxiety neurosis is caused by profound psychological trauma which occurs at birth. 256pp. 5³⁄₈ x 8½.   27974-X

A THEOLOGICO-POLITICAL TREATISE, Benedict Spinoza. Also contains unfinished Political Treatise. Great classic on religious liberty, theory of government on common consent. R. Elwes translation. Total of 421pp. 5⅜ x 8½.   20249-6

CATALOG OF DOVER BOOKS

MY BONDAGE AND MY FREEDOM, Frederick Douglass. Born a slave, Douglass became outspoken force in antislavery movement. The best of Douglass' autobiographies. Graphic description of slave life. 464pp. 5⅜ x 8½. 22457-0

FOLLOWING THE EQUATOR: A Journey Around the World, Mark Twain. Fascinating humorous account of 1897 voyage to Hawaii, Australia, India, New Zealand, etc. Ironic, bemused reports on peoples, customs, climate, flora and fauna, politics, much more. 197 illustrations. 720pp. 5⅜ x 8½. 26113-1

THE PEOPLE CALLED SHAKERS, Edward D. Andrews. Definitive study of Shakers: origins, beliefs, practices, dances, social organization, furniture and crafts, etc. 33 illustrations. 351pp. 5⅜ x 8½. 21081-2

THE MYTHS OF GREECE AND ROME, H. A. Guerber. A classic of mythology, generously illustrated, long prized for its simple, graphic, accurate retelling of the principal myths of Greece and Rome, and for its commentary on their origins and significance. With 64 illustrations by Michelangelo, Raphael, Titian, Rubens, Canova, Bernini and others. 480pp. 5⅜ x 8½. 27584-1

PSYCHOLOGY OF MUSIC, Carl E. Seashore. Classic work discusses music as a medium from psychological viewpoint. Clear treatment of physical acoustics, auditory apparatus, sound perception, development of musical skills, nature of musical feeling, host of other topics. 88 figures. 408pp. 5⅜ x 8½. 21851-1

THE PHILOSOPHY OF HISTORY, Georg W. Hegel. Great classic of Western thought develops concept that history is not chance but rational process, the evolution of freedom. 457pp. 5⅜ x 8½. 20112-0

THE BOOK OF TEA, Kakuzo Okakura. Minor classic of the Orient: entertaining, charming explanation, interpretation of traditional Japanese culture in terms of tea ceremony. 94pp. 5⅜ x 8½. 20070-1

LIFE IN ANCIENT EGYPT, Adolf Erman. Fullest, most thorough, detailed older account with much not in more recent books, domestic life, religion, magic, medicine, commerce, much more. Many illustrations reproduce tomb paintings, carvings, hieroglyphs, etc. 597pp. 5⅜ x 8½. 22632-8

SUNDIALS, Their Theory and Construction, Albert Waugh. Far and away the best, most thorough coverage of ideas, mathematics concerned, types, construction, adjusting anywhere. Simple, nontechnical treatment allows even children to build several of these dials. Over 100 illustrations. 230pp. 5⅜ x 8½. 22947-5

THEORETICAL HYDRODYNAMICS, L. M. Milne-Thomson. Classic exposition of the mathematical theory of fluid motion, applicable to both hydrodynamics and aerodynamics. Over 600 exercises. 768pp. 6⅛ x 9¼. 68970-0

SONGS OF EXPERIENCE: Facsimile Reproduction with 26 Plates in Full Color, William Blake. 26 full-color plates from a rare 1826 edition. Includes "The Tyger," "London," "Holy Thursday," and other poems. Printed text of poems. 48pp. 5¼ x 7. 24636-1

OLD-TIME VIGNETTES IN FULL COLOR, Carol Belanger Grafton (ed.). Over 390 charming, often sentimental illustrations, selected from archives of Victorian graphics—pretty women posing, children playing, food, flowers, kittens and puppies, smiling cherubs, birds and butterflies, much more. All copyright-free. 48pp. 9¼ x 12¼. 27269-9

PERSPECTIVE FOR ARTISTS, Rex Vicat Cole. Depth, perspective of sky and sea, shadows, much more, not usually covered. 391 diagrams, 81 reproductions of drawings and paintings. 279pp. 5⅜ x 8½. 22487-2

DRAWING THE LIVING FIGURE, Joseph Sheppard. Innovative approach to artistic anatomy focuses on specifics of surface anatomy, rather than muscles and bones. Over 170 drawings of live models in front, back and side views, and in widely varying poses. Accompanying diagrams. 177 illustrations. Introduction. Index. 144pp. 8⅜ x11¼. 26723-7

GOTHIC AND OLD ENGLISH ALPHABETS: 100 Complete Fonts, Dan X. Solo. Add power, elegance to posters, signs, other graphics with 100 stunning copyright-free alphabets: Blackstone, Dolbey, Germania, 97 more–including many lower-case, numerals, punctuation marks. 104pp. 8⅛ x 11. 24695-7

HOW TO DO BEADWORK, Mary White. Fundamental book on craft from simple projects to five-bead chains and woven works. 106 illustrations. 142pp. 5⅜ x 8. 20697-1

THE BOOK OF WOOD CARVING, Charles Marshall Sayers. Finest book for beginners discusses fundamentals and offers 34 designs. "Absolutely first rate . . . well thought out and well executed."–E. J. Tangerman. 118pp. 7¾ x 10⅝. 23654-4

ILLUSTRATED CATALOG OF CIVIL WAR MILITARY GOODS: Union Army Weapons, Insignia, Uniform Accessories, and Other Equipment, Schuyler, Hartley, and Graham. Rare, profusely illustrated 1846 catalog includes Union Army uniform and dress regulations, arms and ammunition, coats, insignia, flags, swords, rifles, etc. 226 illustrations. 160pp. 9 x 12. 24939-5

WOMEN'S FASHIONS OF THE EARLY 1900s: An Unabridged Republication of "New York Fashions, 1909," National Cloak & Suit Co. Rare catalog of mail-order fashions documents women's and children's clothing styles shortly after the turn of the century. Captions offer full descriptions, prices. Invaluable resource for fashion, costume historians. Approximately 725 illustrations. 128pp. 8⅜ x 11¼. 27276-1

THE 1912 AND 1915 GUSTAV STICKLEY FURNITURE CATALOGS, Gustav Stickley. With over 200 detailed illustrations and descriptions, these two catalogs are essential reading and reference materials and identification guides for Stickley furniture. Captions cite materials, dimensions and prices. 112pp. 6½ x 9¼. 26676-1

EARLY AMERICAN LOCOMOTIVES, John H. White, Jr. Finest locomotive engravings from early 19th century: historical (1804–74), main-line (after 1870), special, foreign, etc. 147 plates. 142pp. 11⅜ x 8¼. 22772-3

THE TALL SHIPS OF TODAY IN PHOTOGRAPHS, Frank O. Braynard. Lavishly illustrated tribute to nearly 100 majestic contemporary sailing vessels: Amerigo Vespucci, Clearwater, Constitution, Eagle, Mayflower, Sea Cloud, Victory, many more. Authoritative captions provide statistics, background on each ship. 190 black-and-white photographs and illustrations. Introduction. 128pp. 8⅞ x 11¾. 27163-3

LITTLE BOOK OF EARLY AMERICAN CRAFTS AND TRADES, Peter Stockham (ed.). 1807 children's book explains crafts and trades: baker, hatter, cooper, potter, and many others. 23 copperplate illustrations. 140pp. 4⅝ x 6. 23336-7

VICTORIAN FASHIONS AND COSTUMES FROM HARPER'S BAZAR, 1867–1898, Stella Blum (ed.). Day costumes, evening wear, sports clothes, shoes, hats, other accessories in over 1,000 detailed engravings. 320pp. 9⅜ x 12¼. 22990-4

GUSTAV STICKLEY, THE CRAFTSMAN, Mary Ann Smith. Superb study surveys broad scope of Stickley's achievement, especially in architecture. Design philosophy, rise and fall of the Craftsman empire, descriptions and floor plans for many Craftsman houses, more. 86 black-and-white halftones. 31 line illustrations. Introduction 208pp. 6½ x 9¼. 27210-9

THE LONG ISLAND RAIL ROAD IN EARLY PHOTOGRAPHS, Ron Ziel. Over 220 rare photos, informative text document origin (1844) and development of rail service on Long Island. Vintage views of early trains, locomotives, stations, passengers, crews, much more. Captions. 8⅞ x 11¾. 26301-0

VOYAGE OF THE LIBERDADE, Joshua Slocum. Great 19th-century mariner's thrilling, first-hand account of the wreck of his ship off South America, the 35-foot boat he built from the wreckage, and its remarkable voyage home. 128pp. 5⅜ x 8½. 40022-0

TEN BOOKS ON ARCHITECTURE, Vitruvius. The most important book ever written on architecture. Early Roman aesthetics, technology, classical orders, site selection, all other aspects. Morgan translation. 331pp. 5⅜ x 8½. 20645-9

THE HUMAN FIGURE IN MOTION, Eadweard Muybridge. More than 4,500 stopped-action photos, in action series, showing undraped men, women, children jumping, lying down, throwing, sitting, wrestling, carrying, etc. 390pp. 7⅞ x 10⅝. 20204-6 Clothbd.

TREES OF THE EASTERN AND CENTRAL UNITED STATES AND CANADA, William M. Harlow. Best one-volume guide to 140 trees. Full descriptions, woodlore, range, etc. Over 600 illustrations. Handy size. 288pp. 4½ x 6⅜. 20395-6

SONGS OF WESTERN BIRDS, Dr. Donald J. Borror. Complete song and call repertoire of 60 western species, including flycatchers, juncoes, cactus wrens, many more—includes fully illustrated booklet. Cassette and manual 99913-0

GROWING AND USING HERBS AND SPICES, Milo Miloradovich. Versatile handbook provides all the information needed for cultivation and use of all the herbs and spices available in North America. 4 illustrations. Index. Glossary. 236pp. 5⅜ x 8½. 25058-X

BIG BOOK OF MAZES AND LABYRINTHS, Walter Shepherd. 50 mazes and labyrinths in all—classical, solid, ripple, and more—in one great volume. Perfect inexpensive puzzler for clever youngsters. Full solutions. 112pp. 8⅛ x 11. 22951-3

CATALOG OF DOVER BOOKS

PIANO TUNING, J. Cree Fischer. Clearest, best book for beginner, amateur. Simple repairs, raising dropped notes, tuning by easy method of flattened fifths. No previous skills needed. 4 illustrations. 201pp. 5⅜ x 8½. 23267-0

HINTS TO SINGERS, Lillian Nordica. Selecting the right teacher, developing confidence, overcoming stage fright, and many other important skills receive thoughtful discussion in this indispensible guide, written by a world-famous diva of four decades' experience. 96pp. 5⅜ x 8½. 40094-8

THE COMPLETE NONSENSE OF EDWARD LEAR, Edward Lear. All nonsense limericks, zany alphabets, Owl and Pussycat, songs, nonsense botany, etc., illustrated by Lear. Total of 320pp. 5⅜ x 8½. (Available in U.S. only.) 20167-8

VICTORIAN PARLOUR POETRY: An Annotated Anthology, Michael R. Turner. 117 gems by Longfellow, Tennyson, Browning, many lesser-known poets. "The Village Blacksmith," "Curfew Must Not Ring Tonight," "Only a Baby Small," dozens more, often difficult to find elsewhere. Index of poets, titles, first lines. xxiii + 325pp. 5⅝ x 8¼. 27044-0

DUBLINERS, James Joyce. Fifteen stories offer vivid, tightly focused observations of the lives of Dublin's poorer classes. At least one, "The Dead," is considered a masterpiece. Reprinted complete and unabridged from standard edition. 160pp. 5$\frac{3}{16}$ x 8¼. 26870-5

GREAT WEIRD TALES: 14 Stories by Lovecraft, Blackwood, Machen and Others, S. T. Joshi (ed.). 14 spellbinding tales, including "The Sin Eater," by Fiona McLeod, "The Eye Above the Mantel," by Frank Belknap Long, as well as renowned works by R. H. Barlow, Lord Dunsany, Arthur Machen, W. C. Morrow and eight other masters of the genre. 256pp. 5⅜ x 8½. (Available in U.S. only.) 40436-6

THE BOOK OF THE SACRED MAGIC OF ABRAMELIN THE MAGE, translated by S. MacGregor Mathers. Medieval manuscript of ceremonial magic. Basic document in Aleister Crowley, Golden Dawn groups. 268pp. 5⅜ x 8½. 23211-5

NEW RUSSIAN-ENGLISH AND ENGLISH-RUSSIAN DICTIONARY, M. A. O'Brien. This is a remarkably handy Russian dictionary, containing a surprising amount of information, including over 70,000 entries. 366pp. 4½ x 6⅛. 20208-9

HISTORIC HOMES OF THE AMERICAN PRESIDENTS, Second, Revised Edition, Irvin Haas. A traveler's guide to American Presidential homes, most open to the public, depicting and describing homes occupied by every American President from George Washington to George Bush. With visiting hours, admission charges, travel routes. 175 photographs. Index. 160pp. 8¼ x 11. 26751-2

NEW YORK IN THE FORTIES, Andreas Feininger. 162 brilliant photographs by the well-known photographer, formerly with *Life* magazine. Commuters, shoppers, Times Square at night, much else from city at its peak. Captions by John von Hartz. 181pp. 9¼ x 10¾. 23585-8

INDIAN SIGN LANGUAGE, William Tomkins. Over 525 signs developed by Sioux and other tribes. Written instructions and diagrams. Also 290 pictographs. 111pp. 6⅛ x 9¼. 22029-X

ANATOMY: A Complete Guide for Artists, Joseph Sheppard. A master of figure drawing shows artists how to render human anatomy convincingly. Over 460 illustrations. 224pp. 8⅜ x 11¼. 27279-6

MEDIEVAL CALLIGRAPHY: Its History and Technique, Marc Drogin. Spirited history, comprehensive instruction manual covers 13 styles (ca. 4th century through 15th). Excellent photographs; directions for duplicating medieval techniques with modern tools. 224pp. 8⅜ x 11¼. 26142-5

DRIED FLOWERS: How to Prepare Them, Sarah Whitlock and Martha Rankin. Complete instructions on how to use silica gel, meal and borax, perlite aggregate, sand and borax, glycerine and water to create attractive permanent flower arrangements. 12 illustrations. 32pp. 5⅜ x 8½. 21802-3

EASY-TO-MAKE BIRD FEEDERS FOR WOODWORKERS, Scott D. Campbell. Detailed, simple-to-use guide for designing, constructing, caring for and using feeders. Text, illustrations for 12 classic and contemporary designs. 96pp. 5⅜ x 8½.
25847-5

SCOTTISH WONDER TALES FROM MYTH AND LEGEND, Donald A. Mackenzie. 16 lively tales tell of giants rumbling down mountainsides, of a magic wand that turns stone pillars into warriors, of gods and goddesses, evil hags, powerful forces and more. 240pp. 5⅜ x 8½. 29677-6

THE HISTORY OF UNDERCLOTHES, C. Willett Cunnington and Phyllis Cunnington. Fascinating, well-documented survey covering six centuries of English undergarments, enhanced with over 100 illustrations: 12th-century laced-up bodice, footed long drawers (1795), 19th-century bustles, l9th-century corsets for men, Victorian "bust improvers," much more. 272pp. 5⅜ x 8¼. 27124-2

ARTS AND CRAFTS FURNITURE: The Complete Brooks Catalog of 1912, Brooks Manufacturing Co. Photos and detailed descriptions of more than 150 now very collectible furniture designs from the Arts and Crafts movement depict davenports, settees, buffets, desks, tables, chairs, bedsteads, dressers and more, all built of solid, quarter-sawed oak. Invaluable for students and enthusiasts of antiques, Americana and the decorative arts. 80pp. 6½ x 9¼. 27471-3

WILBUR AND ORVILLE: A Biography of the Wright Brothers, Fred Howard. Definitive, crisply written study tells the full story of the brothers' lives and work. A vividly written biography, unparalleled in scope and color, that also captures the spirit of an extraordinary era. 560pp. 6⅛ x 9¼. 40297-5

THE ARTS OF THE SAILOR: Knotting, Splicing and Ropework, Hervey Garrett Smith. Indispensable shipboard reference covers tools, basic knots and useful hitches; handsewing and canvas work, more. Over 100 illustrations. Delightful reading for sea lovers. 256pp. 5⅜ x 8½. 26440-8

FRANK LLOYD WRIGHT'S FALLINGWATER: The House and Its History, Second, Revised Edition, Donald Hoffmann. A total revision–both in text and illustrations–of the standard document on Fallingwater, the boldest, most personal architectural statement of Wright's mature years, updated with valuable new material from the recently opened Frank Lloyd Wright Archives. "Fascinating"–*The New York Times*. 116 illustrations. 128pp. 9¼ x 10¾. 27430-6

PHOTOGRAPHIC SKETCHBOOK OF THE CIVIL WAR, Alexander Gardner. 100 photos taken on field during the Civil War. Famous shots of Manassas Harper's Ferry, Lincoln, Richmond, slave pens, etc. 244pp. 10⅝ x 8¼. 22731-6

FIVE ACRES AND INDEPENDENCE, Maurice G. Kains. Great back-to-the-land classic explains basics of self-sufficient farming. The one book to get. 95 illustrations. 397pp. 5⅜ x 8½. 20974-1

SONGS OF EASTERN BIRDS, Dr. Donald J. Borror. Songs and calls of 60 species most common to eastern U.S.: warblers, woodpeckers, flycatchers, thrushes, larks, many more in high-quality recording. Cassette and manual 99912-2

A MODERN HERBAL, Margaret Grieve. Much the fullest, most exact, most useful compilation of herbal material. Gigantic alphabetical encyclopedia, from aconite to zedoary, gives botanical information, medical properties, folklore, economic uses, much else. Indispensable to serious reader. 161 illustrations. 888pp. 6½ x 9¼. 2-vol. set. (Available in U.S. only.) Vol. I: 22798-7
Vol. II: 22799-5

HIDDEN TREASURE MAZE BOOK, Dave Phillips. Solve 34 challenging mazes accompanied by heroic tales of adventure. Evil dragons, people-eating plants, blood-thirsty giants, many more dangerous adversaries lurk at every twist and turn. 34 mazes, stories, solutions. 48pp. 8¼ x 11. 24566-7

LETTERS OF W. A. MOZART, Wolfgang A. Mozart. Remarkable letters show bawdy wit, humor, imagination, musical insights, contemporary musical world; includes some letters from Leopold Mozart. 276pp. 5⅜ x 8½. 22859-2

BASIC PRINCIPLES OF CLASSICAL BALLET, Agrippina Vaganova. Great Russian theoretician, teacher explains methods for teaching classical ballet. 118 illustrations. 175pp. 5⅜ x 8½. 22036-2

THE JUMPING FROG, Mark Twain. Revenge edition. The original story of The Celebrated Jumping Frog of Calaveras County, a hapless French translation, and Twain's hilarious "retranslation" from the French. 12 illustrations. 66pp. 5⅜ x 8½.
22686-7

BEST REMEMBERED POEMS, Martin Gardner (ed.). The 126 poems in this superb collection of 19th- and 20th-century British and American verse range from Shelley's "To a Skylark" to the impassioned "Renascence" of Edna St. Vincent Millay and to Edward Lear's whimsical "The Owl and the Pussycat." 224pp. 5⅜ x 8½.
27165-X

COMPLETE SONNETS, William Shakespeare. Over 150 exquisite poems deal with love, friendship, the tyranny of time, beauty's evanescence, death and other themes in language of remarkable power, precision and beauty. Glossary of archaic terms. 80pp. 5³⁄₁₆ x 8¼. 26686-9

THE BATTLES THAT CHANGED HISTORY, Fletcher Pratt. Eminent historian profiles 16 crucial conflicts, ancient to modern, that changed the course of civilization. 352pp. 5⅜ x 8½. 41129-X

THE WIT AND HUMOR OF OSCAR WILDE, Alvin Redman (ed.). More than 1,000 ripostes, paradoxes, wisecracks: Work is the curse of the drinking classes; I can resist everything except temptation; etc. 258pp. 5⅜ x 8½. 20602-5

SHAKESPEARE LEXICON AND QUOTATION DICTIONARY, Alexander Schmidt. Full definitions, locations, shades of meaning in every word in plays and poems. More than 50,000 exact quotations. 1,485pp. 6½ x 9¼. 2-vol. set.
Vol. 1: 22726-X
Vol. 2: 22727-8

SELECTED POEMS, Emily Dickinson. Over 100 best-known, best-loved poems by one of America's foremost poets, reprinted from authoritative early editions. No comparable edition at this price. Index of first lines. 64pp. 5$\frac{3}{16}$ x 8¼. 26466-1

THE INSIDIOUS DR. FU-MANCHU, Sax Rohmer. The first of the popular mystery series introduces a pair of English detectives to their archnemesis, the diabolical Dr. Fu-Manchu. Flavorful atmosphere, fast-paced action, and colorful characters enliven this classic of the genre. 208pp. 5$\frac{3}{16}$ x 8¼. 29898-1

THE MALLEUS MALEFICARUM OF KRAMER AND SPRENGER, translated by Montague Summers. Full text of most important witchhunter's "bible," used by both Catholics and Protestants. 278pp. 6⅝ x 10. 22802-9

SPANISH STORIES/CUENTOS ESPAÑOLES: A Dual-Language Book, Angel Flores (ed.). Unique format offers 13 great stories in Spanish by Cervantes, Borges, others. Faithful English translations on facing pages. 352pp. 5⅜ x 8½. 25399-6

GARDEN CITY, LONG ISLAND, IN EARLY PHOTOGRAPHS, 1869–1919, Mildred H. Smith. Handsome treasury of 118 vintage pictures, accompanied by carefully researched captions, document the Garden City Hotel fire (1899), the Vanderbilt Cup Race (1908), the first airmail flight departing from the Nassau Boulevard Aerodrome (1911), and much more. 96pp. 8⅞ x 11¾. 40669-5

OLD QUEENS, N.Y., IN EARLY PHOTOGRAPHS, Vincent F. Seyfried and William Asadorian. Over 160 rare photographs of Maspeth, Jamaica, Jackson Heights, and other areas. Vintage views of DeWitt Clinton mansion, 1939 World's Fair and more. Captions. 192pp. 8⅞ x 11. 26358-4

CAPTURED BY THE INDIANS: 15 Firsthand Accounts, 1750-1870, Frederick Drimmer. Astounding true historical accounts of grisly torture, bloody conflicts, relentless pursuits, miraculous escapes and more, by people who lived to tell the tale. 384pp. 5⅜ x 8½. 24901-8

THE WORLD'S GREAT SPEECHES (Fourth Enlarged Edition), Lewis Copeland, Lawrence W. Lamm, and Stephen J. McKenna. Nearly 300 speeches provide public speakers with a wealth of updated quotes and inspiration–from Pericles' funeral oration and William Jennings Bryan's "Cross of Gold Speech" to Malcolm X's powerful words on the Black Revolution and Earl of Spenser's tribute to his sister, Diana, Princess of Wales. 944pp. 5⅜ x 8⅜. 40903-1

THE BOOK OF THE SWORD, Sir Richard F. Burton. Great Victorian scholar/adventurer's eloquent, erudite history of the "queen of weapons"–from prehistory to early Roman Empire. Evolution and development of early swords, variations (sabre, broadsword, cutlass, scimitar, etc.), much more. 336pp. 6⅛ x 9¼.
25434-8

AUTOBIOGRAPHY: The Story of My Experiments with Truth, Mohandas K. Gandhi. Boyhood, legal studies, purification, the growth of the Satyagraha (nonviolent protest) movement. Critical, inspiring work of the man responsible for the freedom of India. 480pp. 5⅜ x 8½. (Available in U.S. only.) 24593-4

CELTIC MYTHS AND LEGENDS, T. W. Rolleston. Masterful retelling of Irish and Welsh stories and tales. Cuchulain, King Arthur, Deirdre, the Grail, many more. First paperback edition. 58 full-page illustrations. 512pp. 5⅜ x 8½. 26507-2

THE PRINCIPLES OF PSYCHOLOGY, William James. Famous long course complete, unabridged. Stream of thought, time perception, memory, experimental methods; great work decades ahead of its time. 94 figures. 1,391pp. 5⅜ x 8½. 2-vol. set.
Vol. I: 20381-6   Vol. II: 20382-4

THE WORLD AS WILL AND REPRESENTATION, Arthur Schopenhauer. Definitive English translation of Schopenhauer's life work, correcting more than 1,000 errors, omissions in earlier translations. Translated by E. F. J. Payne. Total of 1,269pp. 5⅜ x 8½. 2-vol. set.   Vol. 1: 21761-2   Vol. 2: 21762-0

MAGIC AND MYSTERY IN TIBET, Madame Alexandra David-Neel. Experiences among lamas, magicians, sages, sorcerers, Bonpa wizards. A true psychic discovery. 32 illustrations. 321pp. 5⅜ x 8½. (Available in U.S. only.) 22682-4

THE EGYPTIAN BOOK OF THE DEAD, E. A. Wallis Budge. Complete reproduction of Ani's papyrus, finest ever found. Full hieroglyphic text, interlinear transliteration, word-for-word translation, smooth translation. 533pp. 6½ x 9¼. 21866-X

MATHEMATICS FOR THE NONMATHEMATICIAN, Morris Kline. Detailed, college-level treatment of mathematics in cultural and historical context, with numerous exercises. Recommended Reading Lists. Tables. Numerous figures. 641pp. 5⅜ x 8½. 24823-2

PROBABILISTIC METHODS IN THE THEORY OF STRUCTURES, Isaac Elishakoff. Well-written introduction covers the elements of the theory of probability from two or more random variables, the reliability of such multivariable structures, the theory of random function, Monte Carlo methods of treating problems incapable of exact solution, and more. Examples. 502pp. 5⅜ x 8½. 40691-1

THE RIME OF THE ANCIENT MARINER, Gustave Doré, S. T. Coleridge. Doré's finest work; 34 plates capture moods, subtleties of poem. Flawless full-size reproductions printed on facing pages with authoritative text of poem. "Beautiful. Simply beautiful."—*Publisher's Weekly*. 77pp. 9¼ x 12. 22305-1

NORTH AMERICAN INDIAN DESIGNS FOR ARTISTS AND CRAFTSPEOPLE, Eva Wilson. Over 360 authentic copyright-free designs adapted from Navajo blankets, Hopi pottery, Sioux buffalo hides, more. Geometrics, symbolic figures, plant and animal motifs, etc. 128pp. 8⅜ x 11. (Not for sale in the United Kingdom.) 25341-4

SCULPTURE: Principles and Practice, Louis Slobodkin. Step-by-step approach to clay, plaster, metals, stone; classical and modern. 253 drawings, photos. 255pp. 8⅛ x 11. 22960-2

THE INFLUENCE OF SEA POWER UPON HISTORY, 1660–1783, A. T. Mahan. Influential classic of naval history and tactics still used as text in war colleges. First paperback edition. 4 maps. 24 battle plans. 640pp. 5⅜ x 8½. 25509-3

THE STORY OF THE TITANIC AS TOLD BY ITS SURVIVORS, Jack Winocour (ed.). What it was really like. Panic, despair, shocking inefficiency, and a little heroism. More thrilling than any fictional account. 26 illustrations. 320pp. 5⅜ x 8½. 20610-6

FAIRY AND FOLK TALES OF THE IRISH PEASANTRY, William Butler Yeats (ed.). Treasury of 64 tales from the twilight world of Celtic myth and legend: "The Soul Cages," "The Kildare Pooka," "King O'Toole and his Goose," many more. Introduction and Notes by W. B. Yeats. 352pp. 5⅜ x 8½. 26941-8

BUDDHIST MAHAYANA TEXTS, E. B. Cowell and others (eds.). Superb, accurate translations of basic documents in Mahayana Buddhism, highly important in history of religions. The Buddha-karita of Asvaghosha, Larger Sukhavativyuha, more. 448pp. 5⅜ x 8½. 25552-2

ONE TWO THREE . . . INFINITY: Facts and Speculations of Science, George Gamow. Great physicist's fascinating, readable overview of contemporary science: number theory, relativity, fourth dimension, entropy, genes, atomic structure, much more. 128 illustrations. Index. 352pp. 5⅜ x 8½. 25664-2

EXPERIMENTATION AND MEASUREMENT, W. J. Youden. Introductory manual explains laws of measurement in simple terms and offers tips for achieving accuracy and minimizing errors. Mathematics of measurement, use of instruments, experimenting with machines. 1994 edition. Foreword. Preface. Introduction. Epilogue. Selected Readings. Glossary. Index. Tables and figures. 128pp. 5⅜ x 8½. 40451-X

DALÍ ON MODERN ART: The Cuckolds of Antiquated Modern Art, Salvador Dalí. Influential painter skewers modern art and its practitioners. Outrageous evaluations of Picasso, Cézanne, Turner, more. 15 renderings of paintings discussed. 44 calligraphic decorations by Dalí. 96pp. 5⅜ x 8½. (Available in U.S. only.) 29220-7

ANTIQUE PLAYING CARDS: A Pictorial History, Henry René D'Allemagne. Over 900 elaborate, decorative images from rare playing cards (14th–20th centuries): Bacchus, death, dancing dogs, hunting scenes, royal coats of arms, players cheating, much more. 96pp. 9¼ x 12¼. 29265-7

MAKING FURNITURE MASTERPIECES: 30 Projects with Measured Drawings, Franklin H. Gottshall. Step-by-step instructions, illustrations for constructing handsome, useful pieces, among them a Sheraton desk, Chippendale chair, Spanish desk, Queen Anne table and a William and Mary dressing mirror. 224pp. 8⅛ x 11¼. 29338-6

THE FOSSIL BOOK: A Record of Prehistoric Life, Patricia V. Rich et al. Profusely illustrated definitive guide covers everything from single-celled organisms and dinosaurs to birds and mammals and the interplay between climate and man. Over 1,500 illustrations. 760pp. 7½ x 10⅛. 29371-8

Paperbound unless otherwise indicated. Available at your book dealer, online at **www.doverpublications.com**, or by writing to Dept. GI, Dover Publications, Inc., 31 East 2nd Street, Mineola, NY 11501. For current price information or for free catalogues (please indicate field of interest), write to Dover Publications or log on to **www.doverpublications.com** and see every Dover book in print. Dover publishes more than 500 books each year on science, elementary and advanced mathematics, biology, music, art, literary history, social sciences, and other areas.